# Unfriendly Fire

Singular Lives: The Iowa Series in North American Autobiography

Albert E. Stone, Series Editor

Peg Mullen

# Unfriendly Fire

## A Mother's Memoir

Foreword by Albert E. Stone

UNIVERSITY OF IOWA PRESS  IOWA CITY

University of Iowa Press,
Iowa City 52242

Printed in the United States of America

Design by Richard Hendel



Printed on acid-free paper

Library of Congress
Cataloging-in-Publication Data
Mullen, Peg, 1917–
Unfriendly fire: a mother's memoir /
Peg Mullen; foreword by
Albert E. Stone.
p. cm.—(Singular lives)
ISBN 0-87745-506-6,
ISBN 0-87745-507-4 (pbk.)
1. Vietnamese Conflict, 1961–1975—Protest movements—United States.
2. Vietnamese Conflict, 1961–1975—Casualties (Statistics, etc.). 3. Mullen, Peg, 1917– . 4. Mullen, Michael Eugene, 1944–1970. I. Title. II. Series.
DS559.5.M84 1995
959.704'3373—dc20 94-48108
CIP

*This book is dedicated to the victims of the Vietnam War—of all colors—the millions of young men and women whose lives, limbs, and minds were destroyed by a succession of unscrupulous men in power.*

When the war has ended and the road is open again,
The same stars will course through the heavens.
Then will I weep for the white bones heaped
Together in desolate graves
Of those who sought military honors for their
Leaders.

*From the diary of an unknown North Vietnamese soldier, 1965*

# CONTENTS

# FOREWORD by Albert E. Stone

*Unfriendly Fire* is surely a singular contribution to the discussion, flourishing now for more than two decades, of the meanings of the Vietnam War for American culture. As a mother's memoir, Peg Mullen's autobiography challenges and complements nearly all other voices and viewpoints in this wide-ranging debate. Neither an apologist for the government and military nor a returned veteran, neither a novelist nor a New Journalist, Peg Mullen tells her story simply and passionately as a special witness from the homefront. But hers is not only a mother's voice—muted as these have often been—keening over the loss of nearly 58,000 American lives. Her particular fate has been to be the mother of a soldier killed by friendly fire, dead in his sleep from an artillery shell ostensibly fired in support of the infantry unit of which, on February 18, 1970, Michael E. Mullen was an acting platoon sergeant. Though victims of friendly fire were but one segment of the more than 10,000 nonhostile casualties, their number was never small. Governmental policy and military censorship kept this grisly feature of the conflict as confidential as possible. In part to expose such subterfuges in language and action, but also on behalf of the thousands of American families afflicted by this ironic calamity and, above all, to express her own and her husband's mystified outrage, Peg Mullen has written this eloquent account of one Iowa family's suffering and sacrifice. Her title deliberately unmasks one of her country's more egregious euphemisms of modern warfare.

As the text insistently documents, Peg Mullen not only claims a place in the burgeoning literature of the Vietnam War but also reminds younger readers that her name and activities—though less publicized than those of Jane Fonda and Joan Baez, not to mention Dr. Spock, Abbie Hoffman, or the Berrigan brothers—have been known for a quarter century. First as a state and regional antiwar activist, then in 1976 as the protagonist in C. D. B. Bryan's *Friendly Fire*, her fame extended from her farm near La Porte City, Black Hawk County, Iowa, to the rest of the nation. Even more Americans encountered her resolute personality as translated in 1979 from life to book to TV screen in the prize-winning docudrama *Friendly Fire*, starring Carol Burnett as Peg Mullen.

Given such strategic location within American popular culture and appearing in the afterglow of Desert Storm, *Unfriendly Fire* commands attention to the ongoing task of understanding an increasingly remote and divisive war. Peg Mullen insists, furthermore, upon the need to make personal, moral, and emotional sense rather than articulate more cerebral assessments of historical, political, and sociological causes and consequences. Her valuing personal and familial suffering and resistance makes plain this book's autobiographical theme. For *her* identity becomes *our* shared loss and disillusion amid the mysteries and meanings of one "accidental" death in a far-off war and the accompanying civilian conflicts at home. Their confluence turned Peg and Gene Mullen into confirmed critics of war and the Pentagon, of President Nixon and Colonel Norman Schwarzkopf, Michael Mullen's battalion commander in the hills near Chu Lai.

Their eldest son was in fact and is in memory the apple of his parents' eyes. At the Mullens' story's core, therefore, is Peg's refusal to accept her son's death. Her work's structure reflects the triangular web of relationships among mother, father, son. Michael—small, intense, caring, obedient, hardworking—combined his parents' qualities to become an exemplary Iowa farm child, 4-H member, Catholic high school and college student, reluctant but dutiful draftee. His letters from Vietnam appear as the coda to this family narrative. In understated prose, the soldier repeats the feelings, concerns, and language of other grunts present and dying in more artful accounts like Michael Herr's or Tim O'Brien's. Like them, he records growing bitterness, weariness, and a sense of futility over the search and destroy tactics, the village burnings, the booby traps, and the callous body count preoccupation of his superiors. Gene's secret letter to his dead son—as poignant as any passage in the other Vietnam narratives—dramatizes the silent suffering this father endured as he grieved his way toward acceptance of his son's death.

In between and embracing both dead males' words (for Gene's death came in 1986, before Peg began writing her autobiography) stands the stubbornly honest author-mother-wife. What neither the son's nor the father's letters can reveal is the "truth" of Michael Mullen's killing as a microcosm of the Vietnam War. This quest for wider meaning animated the grieving parents' lives from February 1970 on. Readers of Peg Mullen's story will recognize that the widow, now retired to a modest home in Brownsville, Texas, still pursues the "truth" behind her son's "accidental" killing. This quest becomes inextricably entangled with the mysteries, evasions, obsessions, and the conflicting explanations and blamings surrounding and defining the war. For both parents, *the* cause of Michael Mullen's death must be a personal "Who?" rather than some impersonal concatenation of geography and history, strategy and tactics, mechanical accident or human error. The Mullens' private tragedy and public actions challenge the official justifications, then and later, summarized by Andrew Martin in *Receptions of War: Vietnam in American Culture.* The chief ones were the following: as a "quagmire," Vietnam is to be blamed on no one; the "mystery" that simply happened in a faraway place and time, therefore, defies comprehension; because it became a struggle among "victims," Vietnam "was a war no one won"; and finally the (to some hollow) claim remains that the American military was never actually defeated on the battlefields of Southeast Asia.

Peg Mullen treats such historical explanations simply as excuses rendered suspect or invalid by the testimony in her son's letters and returned soldiers' phone calls, letters, and visits to the farm. Her own preoccupation throughout is with military injustice and political duplicity. What she firmly believes is a conspiracy began the day an officer and her local priest came to the farm to announce, but not honestly explain, Michael's death by friendly fire. Her resistance persists to the present. "I found myself despising everyone in military uniform," she says of her campaign waged through marches and demonstrations, interviews and panels on radio, TV, and in the press, and in reluctant participation in Bryan's writing of *Friendly Fire* and even more reluctant acquiescence to ABC's movie version of her experiences. The final act of remembrance and rebellion, so far at least, is this autobiography.

What is an adequate response to the enormities of this double war—the one in Vietnam and the other on the streets of places like Des Moines and Washington? Peg Mullen's struggle to confront this challenge leads to a bitter cultural diagnosis: the United States has become a thoroughgoing war culture. Further, anyone who dares to declare this "truth" openly risks treatment as an enemy. This threat became reality for her during Nixon's visit to Des Moines in 1971 and her own mauling there at the hands of a plainclothes police officer.

"I desperately need to believe that my son's life was not wasted, that he died for some high ideal." These words were spoken by Peg Mullen in testimony before a congressional committee. When no such ideal emerges, when it becomes clear that, as Gene put it, their son "died for no cause in this conflict with no definition," Peg's crusade concentrates on Colonel (now, of course, General) Schwarzkopf. Desert Storm simply fuels the fires of her righteous indignation. In a later speech at the University of Iowa, "I vented twenty years of dislike for a man who, in my eyes, stood only for war, a man who would win promotion and advancement because of his ability to wage war." Later she rethought these words. "At times I have questioned my own feelings," she states; "the colonel was merely following orders in his mindless pursuit of body count in Vietnam, but I won't forgive his having allowed the sacrifice." When the Gulf War, in its initial stage, produced eleven marines killed by friendly fire, she again felt justified. In an interview on NBC, she declared that "you don't ever come to grips with the loss of a loved one . . . or ever forget—or ever believe there was a reason."

Peg Mullen's recognition of the absence of meaning in her son's and country's fates in Southeast Asia is buttressed by testimony from the web of relationships established with returned veterans and their families, as well as in the personal literature about Vietnam. In *A Rumor of War*, for example, Philip Caputo contrasts "The Nam" and "The World." "On that alien planet," he observes, "no such comforting regularities were discernible. As one soldier commented, 'It was no orderly campaign, as in Europe, but a war waged in a wilderness without rules or laws. . . . Chance. Pure chance. The one true god of modern war is blind chance.'" Brought up, like most of the rest of the "silent majority," to measure issues like war's morality and rational circumstance by the yardstick of World War II, the "Paradigm War," the Mullens were bitter, confused, yearned fiercely for meaning. *Unfriendly Fire* documents such cultural and personal despair with convincing clarity and force.

For many knowledgeable readers, Peg Mullen's heroic, intense struggle to impose meaning on a son's death and a disastrous war reinforces insights already received through other channels. This book's title and narrative focus inevitably recall Bryan's *Friendly Fire*. The contrast between an inside autobiographical narrative and a presumably "objective" or outside account is instructive in many ways, many of which are too intricate to be disentangled here. What is clear from Peg Mullen's version is her utter reliance upon personal experience and belief. The *New Yorker* writer's story, however, asserts that, while "truth" may never be forthcoming in Michael Mullen's case, it can be approached by curiosity, care, and sympathetic weighing of various views and personal investments in available facts and explanations. When Peg and Gene Mullen became disenchanted with *Friendly Fire*, it was only partly because the writer from down in Iowa City had listened carefully to many versions of Michael Mullen's killing—including at some length Colonel Schwarzkopf's. More basic still was their conviction that "during the five years he worked on our story, it simply became his story, and we definitely did not like his version." As Gene Mullen remarked to Bryan, "You wanted the story, and we wanted the truth." To which Bryan added, "They were right." Assembling and assessing the facts about the past could not produce "truth" until the story was *possessed*—made, that is, meaningful by both actors and the teller.

*Unfriendly Fire* implicitly affirms this conflict between "telling the truth" and "telling a story." Nonetheless, Peg Mullen remains true to her self—a brave, determined, honest, deeply scarred mother. Writing her son's story as advocate and witness re-establishes, indeed, creates, her autobiographical identity. It becomes a way out of grief while keeping Michael Mullen alive in memory and imagination. The son who died needlessly in Vietnam keeps whispering to her, "Don't give up. Protest this war."

# INTRODUCTION

In 1968 my son Michael was drafted and one year later he was sent to Vietnam. He was killed in February 1970 in one of the longest military engagements in the history of our country. The United States became involved in the conflict between North and South Vietnam after the French lost the war in 1954. Earlier, President Truman had sent financial aid to South Vietnam to stem Communism. In 1955 President Eisenhower introduced military personnel to help train the South Vietnamese army, followed by the deployment of American troops during the Kennedy years. In 1964, after Kennedy's assassination, President Johnson presented the U.S. Senate with the Gulf of Tonkin resolution, enabling him to expand our involvement into a full-fledged military action. Only two senators voted against the amendment, Ernest Gruening of Alaska and Wayne Morse of Oregon. By 1969 we had 540,000 troops fighting and dying in a country 10,000 miles from our shores.

President Nixon campaigned in the 1968 election on a platform to end the war, an issue that he put aside immediately following his election. With the aid of his secretary of state, Henry Kissinger, who talked about a negotiated peace for five years, the U.S. finally reached an agreement in March 1973 with the North Vietnamese. Our troops were withdrawn in disgrace and defeat. The war continued until 1975, when Saigon fell to the Communists from the north.

During these years my husband, Gene, and I lived on a small farm in Black Hawk County, Iowa. The farm didn't produce enough income to support our family of four, so Gene worked off the farm at the John Deere Tractor Works in nearby Waterloo. The job enabled us to forge ahead in improving the farm, send our children to a private college-prep high school, then to college and graduate school.

On February 18, 1970, Michael was killed in Vietnam by friendly fire. When I learned of his death two days later, I had no time to grieve. By the time his body arrived home, I had waged a nine-day battle with the military establishment, and after his burial I made a decision to continue the struggle. I embarked on a campaign that lasted until the Vietnam War finally ended five years later.

My frenzied activities during those years were documented in March 1976 by author C. D. B. Bryan in three issues of the *New Yorker* and released in book form by Putnam Publishers that April, entitled *Friendly Fire.* In April 1979 a movie of the same name, based on the book, was produced by Marble Arch Productions and aired on ABC-TV with Carol Burnett playing the lead role. The production won six Emmys. It documented my fight to learn the truth about my son's death by friendly fire, resulting in my personal struggle to bring the Vietnam War to an end.

For the past twenty-four years I have lived with the term "friendly fire." I first became aware of it when a military officer handed me a telegram telling me that my son had died in Vietnam as a result of friendly fire. My reaction was immediate: anger and disbelief. Then I asked questions and learned the term was used to describe military casualties caused by "friends."

The term continues to haunt me. How can military men and women on duty in a war zone have their deaths described as friendly? The term has grown more popular as we continue to become involved in war after war, each of them producing more friendly fire deaths than the last. Some scholars are now writing that *all* U.S. casualties in the recent Gulf War were from friendly fire.

It is time to eliminate this term from our military linguistics. A military death during a war is a war casualty not a friendly affair.

The magazine articles, the book, the movie, our antiwar ad and several years of news items in the *Des Moines Register*, and personal appearances by me combined to produce a cascade of mail. Letters came from war victims who suddenly were speaking out: the veterans themselves; bereaved mothers, fathers, sisters, and brothers; children deprived of their fathers; and bewildered grandparents.

These often poetic communications contain the only true account of those dark years and the havoc our military inflicted on households across the United States. They convinced me that I needed to tell our story, as that of only one family of the forgotten people in the Vietnam War. I have quoted from only a few of the letters, but all have been preserved in the Women's Archives at the University of Iowa Libraries, Iowa City, Iowa.

I want to thank the wonderful people who cared and who took a few moments to let my family know.

# ACKNOWLEDGMENTS

This book could not have been written without the help of the Elderhostel Summer Program associated with the Iowa Writers' Workshop at the University of Iowa. I attended four sessions of memoirs writing from 1990 to 1993.

Many thanks to Peg Houston, director of the Elderhostel. Special thanks to Chris Offutt, my first instructor, who refused to give up on me.

Thanks to John Staggs and Dan McClanahan, young newspaper reporters in southern Texas, who read and edited my first bulky manuscript.

My sincere gratitude to Fritz McDonald, a graduate of the Writers' Workshop and a professor at Kirkwood College in Cedar Rapids, Iowa, who offered his talented services to me for a final editing. He never wavered in his support and enthusiasm.

And special thanks to Bob Burchfield, assigned to me as editor, soft-voiced and humble, who had no trouble convincing me to make a change.

Thanks to my three children, Patricia, Mary, and John, who encouraged me to write my story and listened patiently while I talked about little else for four years.

# ONE : OCTOBER 16, 1989

It was a quiet night on my street in Brownsville, Texas. The windows and doors were open to let in the gulf breeze. Three years had passed since my husband's death and my decision to go it alone in Texas.

I was stretched out in a La-Z-Boy chair enjoying the second game of the World Series between the Oakland A's and the San Francisco Giants. Suddenly the telephone rang. All bells and alarms in our home had always been loud because of my husband's deafness. I had grown used to them. The phone rang twice before I reached it.

"Hello," I said.

Several seconds elapsed without a response. Not wanting to miss a moment of the series, I said, "What's your problem?"

The caller stammered, then asked to speak to Gene Mullen. I explained that he had died in 1986. He asked for Peg.

I identified myself, and without further hesitation he blurted out, "I'm the man who killed your son in Vietnam nineteen years ago."

I was stunned—this was the call I had waited for since 1970. I thought of Gene and thanked God he was not sitting in his chair—he couldn't have handled any more grief.

Then my concern turned to the anguished man on the phone: "Why are you calling me at this late date? And how did you get my telephone number?"

Regaining his composure, he replied, "I've always known where you were. My buddy who was with me in Vietnam that night was from Iowa and lived only about forty miles north of your farm."

I told him I'd known for many years of the existence of his friend. Rick, a Vietnam veteran who had gone to high school with some of my children, came to see me one morning several months after Michael's death. He wanted to tell me about drinking beer in a tavern in Waterloo the evening before with a veteran who had served in the artillery unit responsible for our son's death. Rick did not learn his name and never saw the man again. It would have been difficult for us to locate the veteran; we understood why he had not contacted us, so we made no effort to find him.

"I'm calling for many reasons," he continued. "First you must know that the men in the 14th Artillery were not drinking as shown in *Friendly Fire*. We'd been asleep for several hours when we were awakened shortly after 2 A.M. by our lieutenant with orders to fire the guns."

When an infantry unit was on a mission in the jungle, far from its home base, it was the responsibility of the artillery to provide cover in case of enemy attack. As soon as the infantry dug in for the night, an artillery officer (forward observer) who traveled with them radioed their location back to his headquarters. Meticulous calculations were made between the forward observer and the officer in charge of the 105-mm howitzers. When everyone involved was satisfied that the coordinates were perfect, the men who would fire the guns, if necessary, were informed of the three numbers that would be punched in at the gun sight.

My caller continued: "Exact location of Charlie Company had been determined earlier in the evening, the coordinates were set, and everything was ready in case the infantry came under attack. We were told the test rounds had been cancelled and we could go to bed."

For years we tried to find out whose decision it was to call in the artillery cover at 2:30 A.M. when no enemy action had been reported and the men were asleep in their foxholes. Several GIs who had been there told me it was a standing order to awaken the men when the artillery would go over their position.

He hesitated for a moment, then continued: "A slip of paper on which three numbers had been handwritten was handed to me by the artillery officer who woke us up—the numbers were the coordinates that had been set into the gun earlier in the evening. As my buddy and I approached the howitzer, both of us were groggy. I looked closely at the note in my hand and without hesitation punched the three numbers into the artillery piece. Now, fully awake, I knew the third number was wrong."

The tragic error resulted in the wounding of six men by shrapnel, the instant death of my son Michael, when a small piece of steel pierced his heart, and the death of a young man from West Virginia who died twenty-four hours later.

"Mrs. Mullen, both of us buried the incident deep in our minds—neither of us wanted to face the havoc and terror we must have caused. It was not until the book was published that we knew real people died that night. Mrs. Mullen, I can't keep this secret any longer. I flashback night after night. My buddy from Iowa often comes to see me, and for years we've wanted to call you."

It must have taken a great deal of courage for the caller to tell me his story. After years of conversations with veterans, I understood why he hadn't called sooner. Most of them first had to heal emotionally, and it took years. At this moment I felt it was necessary for me to ease his hurt.

"Maybe it will help you to know," I said, "that many years ago we heard that an officer in the artillery had been reprimanded, in fact had been court-martialed. We have no proof because the Defense Department has refused for nineteen years to release the investigation of Michael's death. You were not guilty, nor was your friend. So now maybe life will be easier for you."

The passage in *Friendly Fire* accusing the men in the 14th Artillery of drunkenness was not our story. It came from Colonel Norman Schwarzkopf, commanding officer of Charlie Company of the 198th

Battalion. At the time of the misfire he was asleep on the hill with the artillery. When checking his unit the next morning, he was quick to tell them that he saw empty beer cans stacked in front of the howitzers. None of the men who came back alive from his company understood why the CO told them this story; they were consumed with anger which didn't need to be reenforced.

I thanked the veteran for calling. I didn't ask his name but assured him that I believed his story. I wished him peace of mind and hung up.

Nineteen years of letters, phone calls, and visits from Vietnam veterans had insulated me. I had learned to live with "friendly fire"—the book, the movie, and the colonel. I could not forget that period in my life, but grieving was in the past. I made myself a cup of coffee and returned to the world of baseball.

The next morning I felt impelled to call Courty Bryan, the author of *Friendly Fire*, and tell him that part of the mystery of Michael's death had been made clear at last. I added that I believed the caller's version of what happened, but there remained too many unanswered questions.

"Who called in the artillery without alerting the sleeping men in their foxholes?" I asked. "It was the duty of the forward observer to do so; he hadn't failed them in the past—why that night? And why was it called in when there was no enemy activity in the area?" Bryan listened politely but didn't seem interested in the news. He asked about my health and thanked me for calling.

Gene and I never believed Colonel Schwarzkopf's story that the misfire was the result of the men being drunk; we didn't believe Bryan's conclusion that the artillery had failed to take the height of the trees into consideration. Gene had come to the conclusion that someone failed to load the proper number of canisters into the gun, causing a shortfall, i.e., the trajectory did not reach the height or length to avoid the sleeping men on the ground.

In February 1991, twenty-one years after Michael's death, I found myself caught up in a new war, Desert Storm, and another incident of friendly fire involving troops under the command of the same Vietnam colonel, now wearing four stars and known as "Stormin' Norman" Schwarzkopf.

The general had ordered twelve marines under his command into the desert to engage enemy tanks. This was done before the high command had issued orders for the start of ground warfare. The marines were mistaken for the enemy by the general's own air power, and eleven died when they were bombed.

For years I had attempted to obtain a copy of the official investigation of Michael's death, and in the fall of 1990 I tried once again through the Freedom of Information Act. I was referred to department after department in the Pentagon. Finally, I heard the last word from the National Archives. Michael's file had reached them, minus the investigation report. They explained that very few investigation reports accompanied the records of Vietnam casualties that the archives received from the army.

There must have been thousands of deaths subject to investigation during our country's ten-year involvement in Vietnam. Statistics published years later indicated that more than 10,000 casualties were caused by accidents, murder, friendly fire, drug overdose, and other unexplained causes, all labeled nonhostile deaths.

For centuries it has been necessary to sanitize all wars and their records.

# TWO : MICHAEL

When Michael Mullen was killed he was known only to his family and a close circle of friends. As a young adult he had not ventured very far from Iowa—only to Rockhurst College in Kansas City and the University of Missouri in Columbia. His flight on a troop carrier to Vietnam must have traumatized his very soul.

Because his father and mother, with the assistance of C. D. B. Bryan, made his death by friendly fire a crusade to awaken all fathers and mothers to the insanity of war, he is remembered by a nation.

Michael was forced into manhood as a little boy because of the circumstances in which he grew up. His father returned from World

War II and bought the family farm near La Porte City, Iowa. Following his service in the Mexican War, Michael's great-great-grandfather, John Dobshire, purchased the farm in 1854 from the federal government. As it passed from one generation to another, it had been allowed to deteriorate. The farm consisted of 120 acres, 110 acres for crops (corn and soybeans) and 10 acres of grassland for grazing cattle. Our first crop harvested in 1946 yielded only 35 bushels of corn per acre, compared to 175 bushels today. Gene realized it would not support our family, so he went to work off the farm. For eighteen years he farmed and also worked eight hours a day at the Rath Packing Company, then the John Deere Tractor Works, both in Waterloo. Michael was a fidgety youngster—never sitting still—a natural for doing lightweight farm chores as soon as he could grip the handle of a small pail.

Michael was born September 11, 1944, in Des Moines, Iowa, and learned to walk at Fort Logan, Colorado, where his father was stationed. At that time the army base was an oasis at the foot of the Rockies—it was called the country club of the U.S. Army. Gene was in charge of the mess hall, and all the cooks and bakers were German prisoners.

I went regularly to the mess hall to eat and, while there, would allow older prisoners—fathers and grandfathers—to play with Michael. It was against military code, but I didn't care. In the safety of the storeroom one elderly man would toss Michael into the air and nearly hug the life out of him. Another would hold the year-old baby close to his shoulder and croon a German lullaby. My heart went out to these soldiers, whom I saw as victims of Hitler and his government.

After we moved to the farm near La Porte City in the spring of 1946, Michael had the privilege of spending his third and fourth years with a grandfather who came to live with us. I had been living with my father, Clair Goodyear, in Des Moines when Michael was born, so the two were meeting again. Unfortunately, Michael's father had little time to spare. As long as his grandfather lived, Michael called him Dad and his father Gene.

Every evening during the summer months Grandfather Goodyear, followed by his grandson, walked a half mile down the road to the pasture to bring back the cows to be milked by Gene when he came home. Mikey, emulating his grandfather every step of the way,

*Our farm home near La Porte City, Iowa, August 1978, with our dog, Sandy. The land had been in Gene's family since the 1850s, and we moved to the farm in 1946. Gene drew the plans for the house, which we built in 1961.*

carried a stick as big as himself, chased the cows in and out of the ditches, guided them into the barn, and finished the job by standing on his toes and reaching high to latch the barn door. When Grandpa came in for dinner in the evening, he loved to recount events of their trip to the pasture and back.

Michael was almost six when he started school in September 1950, getting on the school bus at the early hour of 7:30. He attended the public school in La Porte City, a town of about two thousand at that time. The town had its beginnings in the 1850s and over the years became a thriving community. It sold every commodity a farming community needed and at one time had the largest canning factory in the state, canning sweet corn. It had a railroad, the Rock Island,

and a commuter trolley, the WCFN, which ran every hour, carrying farm children to high school in Waterloo and laborers to work at the Rath Packing Company and the John Deere Tractor Works. Soon city buses served the public in Cedar Falls and Waterloo, motor cars replaced the horse and buggy, and the trolley was abandoned. Businesses began to fade with the Great Depression, and La Porte became a bedroom town.

Michael was small when he started school, but that didn't keep him from getting into trouble on the playground during the first couple of weeks. His only preschool friend, a mean little kid, was twice his size, so Michael learned early to defend himself. On the playground, he was pushed and shoved around by the bigger boys, who were delighted when he responded. He came home with buttons off and knees out of new jeans.

One day I admonished him to stop fighting. He promised to behave, then got off the school bus the next afternoon with a scratch on his cheek and a torn shirt collar. Before I could say a word he looked at me wide-eyed and said, "Mom, I kept my promise, I stopped fighting—but they didn't."

La Porte City Grade School had an excellent arts and crafts show each year for all classes, and the competition among students was intense. Michael, in the first grade, had worked hard on a sculpture of a baby pig molded out of Play-Doh—he was positive he had a winner. When the students were taken to the gymnasium to view the exhibit and check out the winners, he was incensed to learn that he did not receive the best in his class. He immediately approached a neighbor and asked who judged the contest. When Beverly replied that she had, he remarked in disgust, "No wonder I didn't win—just a bunch of farmwives as judges." The competitive spirit shown by the undersized seven-year-old stayed with him as he grew to adulthood. He thrived on competition; however, he learned to accept defeat graciously.

When Michael turned eight, I was about to have my fourth child in five years. He had been an only child for almost four years. Naturally he was upset. One evening we sat on the davenport and talked about it.

"Mom, why are you having babies all the time?" he asked. "We don't have room for another. We don't have any money. What I'm trying to say is that mothers of my friends on the school bus don't

*Our children in 1955. Clockwise from left: Michael, eleven; Patricia, eight; John, three; and Mary, five.*

have babies every year." This astute little eight-year-old thought for a moment and added, "Why don't you ask Dr. Paige about it. I'm sure there must be a pill he could give you." Years later, while studying biochemistry in graduate school, he laughed and said, "Mom, at eight I knew the pill was the most perfect drug ever discovered."

Small and uncoordinated, Michael was not good at sports, but that didn't dampen his enthusiasm. At twelve, he and his friend Jack erected a basketball backboard in the backyard. They used discarded telephone poles, purchased for one dollar each; somehow these young boys were able to get them into the ground, standing straight and sturdy. The backboard was regulation size, and the height of the hoop was perfect. Their fathers once asked them how long they thought it would stand. In disgust Jack replied, "You wait and see." It stood, with a new paint job when needed, for thirty-five years. Hours and hours of one-on-one basketball were played while Michael and John, his brother, were growing up.

Michael loved to play golf and started as soon as he was old enough to drive to the golf course near La Porte City. John joined him when he was ten and in two or three years was able to beat his older brother. Eventually, Michael played basketball in junior high and high school but couldn't do better than the second team. He happily settled for a less glamorous role and played with spirit.

From a young age Michael knew he would go to college. As he grew up, he worked whenever he could to earn his way. On his first job, at age eleven, he cut asparagus on a farm two miles away. He got up at 5 A.M., pedaled his bike to the farm, and cut for two hours before school. Then he would hurry home to eat breakfast and catch the school bus. He earned about forty dollars each spring and banked every penny of it. Workers were paid by the weight of each basket picked, and through this method of payment he was introduced to dishonesty on the job for the first time in his life. One of the young pickers bragged about putting sand in his basket, then covering it with asparagus. Michael was so upset he talked about this every morning for quite some time.

4-H clubs were wonderful outlets for farm boys and girls, enabling them to reach out to new friends and easing their isolation. They had goals every summer and projects that were absorbing. Each of the boys groomed an animal to show at the county fair; some girls also opted for animals—others prepared clothing and baked goods.

One of the activities of each local township group was to tour the farms to inspect the animals being readied for the county fair. While preparing for one of the annual tours, Michael spent the evening scrubbing his steer and grooming it for the next day's visitors. He tied it in the barn so it would stay in tip-top condition.

When it came time to bring the steer out into the farm lot so the visitors could view it, it wouldn't budge. Michael had the lead rope around the animal's neck, pulling with all his strength, with one foot

*Michael at age eleven, with one of his 4-H projects.*

braced against the open barn door. His buddy was on the other end, twisting the critter's tail and pushing. A photographer with the *Waterloo Courier* snapped a picture at just the right moment. The Associated Press picked it up and distributed it nationwide, bearing the title, "Something's got to give."

When Michael died he was remembered by Connie Barker, a friend from 4-H days and now an attorney in Sacramento, California:

> Michael and I met in high school when we were both delegates to the 4-H leadership camp. His high school graduation picture is on the first page of my photo album. . . . He wrote on the back, "Connie, think not that time is an endless, vast creation, for what we do now will set the road for the future. Be sure that you set your road high and straight with no diversions of purpose in it. If you can't make heads or tails of the above, don't worry, I can't either"—so like Michael.

*This photograph of twelve-year-old Michael trying to drag his steer out of the barn, which first appeared in a local newspaper, was picked up by the Associated Press and distributed nationally with the caption, "Something's got to give."*

Phyllis, a neighbor who had started school with Michael, sitting on the bus with him through grade school, sent a sympathy card and enclosed a handwritten note: "I think I had a crush on him from the day we started kindergarten."

One foggy night during Michael's fourteenth summer, we were awakened by the sound of voices approaching the house. Soon there was a knock at our back door, and when I opened it I found a man lying on the porch, covered with blood. I called for Gene and Michael.

Michael took charge and asked me for towels and all the ice I could find in the freezer. He then packed the injured man's face with ice, handing me the bloody towels to rinse in cold water. Meanwhile, I was trying to persuade the local doctor to come. He referred to our victim as "just another drunk" and told me to call the Highway Patrol. He also informed me that people didn't die from loss of blood as a result of facial cuts.

After fifteen minutes of trying to stem the bleeding, the injured man spoke out: "Don't you know me Mike, I'm Don." Another quick call to the doctor to tell him the injured man was our close friend and neighbor. This time he responded, "I'll be there in ten minutes with an ambulance."

The doctor called us the next day to say that it had taken two doctors six hours to put in 350 stitches. He added that they would have been unable to make the repairs if Michael hadn't packed Don's face in ice.

Two days after Michael's death was announced we received a letter from the injured neighbor, scrawled on tablet paper.

> Gene, Peg and family:
>
> It isn't that I couldn't afford a card—I couldn't find one that would express my feelings. . . .
>
> You were always the best neighbors we had—Evelyn and I—I don't intend to forget it. Gene, if you need a pallbearer I will be available. Just call, my boys Rick and Dan would be grateful to help out. We owe you so much.
>
> Yours truly,
> Don Elliott and family

Michael loved school—spent hours studying as he grew older. From the first Iowa Basic Skills tests in third grade it became apparent he was destined for a different life than the farm offered. We agonized about where to send him for high school. Our local school system, at that time, did not push college and did little to obtain scholarships for worthy students. Scholarships, however, were to become important in Michael's future. We were excited when we learned that the Dubuque Catholic Diocese planned to build a central high school in our area. Don Bosco High School, in Gilbertville, had been operating six or seven years when Michael entered as a freshman, taking the college prep course it offered.

He graduated in the top 5 percent of his class and was awarded a scholarship to Rockhurst College in Kansas City, Missouri. He originally planned to study law but was encouraged by Dr. Oscar Wright to study biochemistry. However, Michael's first love was history, and with the permission of his chemistry professor and the college board, he was allowed to carry a double major, the second, the study of history.

The summer preceding his senior year in college Michael bought his first car—a used one—and paid $500 for it. When at home, he spent every free moment polishing this prize. We parked it in the backyard when he left for Vietnam. It sat there for almost a year after his death. No one had the heart to sell it. One day, while alone, I called a friend who had a tow truck and asked him to come and get it.

Upon graduating from Rockhurst College with honors, Michael was offered three fellowships: one to the University of Minnesota, one to the University of Oklahoma, and one to the University of Missouri. He settled on the University of Missouri because he had been in the state during the previous four years and liked it.

Many times during the past twenty-four years I've wondered what would have happened to him if he had chosen one of the other colleges. The head of his department at Missouri served on volunteer committees at the personal request of President Nixon and supported the war.

Michael had been in graduate school about six weeks when he called home one night, depressed and worried about not making the grade. I counseled him to put the books aside for an evening, buy a six-pack of beer, and drink all six cans. When I left the phone, I turned around to face sixteen-year-old John, who laughingly said, "Mom, I'll bet you're the only mother in the state to advise her son to drink a six-pack of beer." Michael followed my advice and it worked. He conquered organic chemistry.

The entire family looked forward to Michael's visits home during the holidays. He always brought someone home with him; today these young men are all my adopted sons. Our daughters, Patricia and Mary, who were in high school at Don Bosco, welcomed the male visitors. Since Michael's friends were from the city, it was a treat for them to visit a farm and help with the cattle and hog chores. Gene was still working off the farm, so when Michael left for college, John, at the age of twelve, had to fill his brother's shoes.

Michael's enthusiasm for life never left him, and we spent hours talking during these visits. His dad used to remark, "How can you and Michael talk all night—don't you ever run out of words?" Conversation around the dinner table was always lively and quite often heated. Political issues were always a main topic, and during the turbulent years of the sixties the pros and cons of every candidate were discussed repeatedly.

We were stunned when President Johnson announced he would not run for another term. There had been rumors he was on the verge of making peace with North Vietnam. However, we were positive the public would demand that a new president bring a quick halt to the carnage in Vietnam. Although we were strong Democrats in a Republican community and state, I was unhappy with Senator Hubert Humphrey's run for the presidency in 1968. But all of us were sickened when we learned that Richard Nixon would be his opponent. At one point Michael remarked that the only man in the country who would get us out of the war was Senator Barry Goldwater.

Michael had to register for the draft during his senior year in high school. He obtained a deferment to attend college, and for the next five years the draft board was a constant presence in his life. It was necessary to renew his deferment year after year, but when he obtained permission to attend graduate school he began to relax. He felt biochemistry was a vital field, and he gambled that a change of president would bring the war to an end. He'd had no draft counseling and didn't have the upbringing to run away.

In September of 1968 the Black Hawk County Draft Board refused to renew Michael's deferment. He asked for an extension so he could present his completed thesis for a master's degree, but his request was refused. He tried to enlist in the Air Force and passed all the tests, but there were no openings for three months. Again the draft board refused a stay.

Michael was sent to Fort Polk, Louisiana, to train in the infantry. Almost immediately the army put pressure on him to go to officer's training school. He refused several times and was told he would be sent to the jungle at the end of his basic training. To stall these orders he applied for noncommissioned officer's training. He was accepted and spent the next six months at Fort Benning, Georgia, graduating with the rank of sergeant. At the end of the specialized training he knew he had lost the gamble. Nixon had been elected president, and in a few short days he'd forgotten his promise to end the war. Michael also realized that his years of schooling meant nothing to the infantry and its officers.

When Michael died, Dr. Wright, the chemistry professor who had become his close friend, wrote from a college in Louisiana to the chair of the history department at Rockhurst College, telling how deeply he felt the loss. He included a substantial check and a request that the department purchase reference books in history and have them inscribed: "In memory of Mike Mullen, killed in action in Vietnam, February 18, 1970, a chemistry major who, in the true liberal arts tradition, was very fond of history."

# THREE : YOUR SON IS DEAD

Saturday morning, February 21, 1970; a beautiful, crisp day in Iowa. A layer of fresh snow covered the eyesores of winter on the farm. Our home, built in 1961 and painted red-brown, stood out in stark contrast. The dozens of evergreen trees, scattered around the homestead, added to its beauty. I awoke early, feeling strangely refreshed. I couldn't understand my serenity. The two previous days had been spent in utter turmoil.

Michael had been in Vietnam almost six months, assigned to the Americal Division based at Chu Lai, a hamlet located in I Corps. The U.S. military command had divided Vietnam into four corps for identification. I Corps bordered the enemy territory on the north. Michael had spent all but six days in country, "humping" through the jungle day and night. Humping was a slang term used by the foot soldier who walked on a mission, carrying everything he needed on his back. The Americal Division was not an elite unit, so it rarely had helicopters available.

Michael's commanding officers clear to the top commander, General Creighton Abrams, were obsessed with the need to increase "body count," a designation representing the number of enemy killed on any mission. It was a policy instigated by General William Westmoreland when he was in command of the Vietnam theater. The strategy became the major criterion to evaluate the performance of a commanding officer, and it took its toll on the ordinary foot soldier.

The last time I'd talked to my son had been by short wave from Vietnam a week earlier. The phone had rung late at night. I picked up the receiver and was elated when the operator asked if I would accept a call from Michael. He told me he had come down from his firebase to pick up a new lieutenant in Chu Lai. He'd had the opportunity to get a haircut and mentioned that he had gone to headquarters to withdraw his savings and send it home. I called his brother to the telephone, and when John handed it back to me I heard: "Mom, it is so sticky here, so bad here. Good-bye."

On Thursday I had awakened with a dreadful foreboding, and as the day wore on it became worse. I couldn't understand what was wrong. I'd worked at my sewing machine all day, trying to overcome the feeling that the bottom was dropping out of my world. I cried incessantly—each new stitch of the drapes I was making was bathed with a tear.

Friday proved to be even gloomier. My tears had given way to anger. I was confused and violently upset. I fought with my husband until he left for his job, working second shift at the John Deere Tractor Works in Waterloo. Shortly after he'd left the house, I decided to drive to Cedar Falls to visit a close friend. Mary was someone with whom I had worked ten years earlier. We both hated the war, and she was faced with the worry of a young son approaching draft age. I didn't tell her why I had come. The afternoon was spent in good conversation and music. Mary was an accomplished organist who always welcomed an audience.

Arriving home before dark, I looked around the house and compulsively put it in order. I scrubbed, dusted, ran the vacuum. The 10 P.M. news was bad. I remember distinctly the account of an accidental shelling by the ARVN (Army of the Republic of Vietnam, an ally of the United States) on Bien Hoa, with many Americans killed and wounded. I didn't wait up for Gene. I fell asleep with the strange thought that my house was in order and I was ready—for what I did not know.

Now it was Saturday morning. After breakfast Gene went out to the hog house to spend the day as a farmer. He loved farming and every day regretted that it was a part-time occupation. I went to the basement hideaway off the family room and sat down to my sewing machine to finish the draperies. This was the spot where I found contentment in any difficult situation. My tears and anger had vanished.

Suddenly the back door crashed open, and I heard my husband's anguished cry.

"It's Mikey! It's Mikey! He's dead!"

At that moment I knew what had been wrong with my Thursday and Friday. I reached for a small bottle near my typewriter and swallowed a Valium. My dear country doctor had insisted that I keep them near me while Michael was in Vietnam, "just in case." I remained calm as I walked upstairs to face a young marine sergeant and our local priest.

The two men stood by and did nothing as Gene vented his rage, beating the walls, accusing the priest of not speaking out against the evils of this war. He picked up a chair, and for a moment I thought he would break the large picture window that overlooked his treasured acres. Instead, he wilted in grief. He sat at the kitchen table, his shoulders heaving with sobs, his white head cradled in his folded arms.

I turned to the sergeant—I'll never forget his eyes. Was the agony reflected in them for Gene and me, or was it the culmination of having delivered one too many death messages? I asked to see the telegram in his hand. I read: "General Wingate regrets to inform you that Michael Mullin died as a result of friendly fire at 2:30 A.M. February 18, 1970, near Tam Ky City, Vietnam." Mullen had been misspelled. This was the first of many insults we experienced in the coming days.

"Good God, you didn't even allow him the decency of dying at the hands of the enemy," I said. Our son's life had been taken for no reason in a war without definition.

I remembered Michael's telephone call in September of 1968 from draft headquarters in Des Moines. While waiting for the fog to lift before flying on to Fort Polk, he'd spent two days in the office working on files. There he'd read with amazement how easily he could have evaded the draft.

"Mom, don't stop fighting this war," he'd said. "You know I don't need to be here. I didn't need to be drafted."

Living on a farm in a conservative community in the heartland of America, we were almost completely untouched by the antiwar movement along the East and West coasts. My activities against the war consisted mostly of flooding Congress and the White House with pleas to end the war. I was active in the Democratic Party at the county and state levels, following campaigns of those who expressed their dislike of the Vietnam War. We had heated arguments during the 1968 campaign; the children and I were for Senator Eugene McCarthy—Gene favored Senator Hubert Humphrey. We despaired at the election of Nixon.

I asked the sergeant to explain the phrase "friendly fire" and why the word "accidental" was not in the message.

"Because it was not accidental," he said. He talked about the shelling of Bien Hoa and how he assumed Michael had been killed there. I immediately knew he had no information (only what he, too, had heard on the news) and would be unable to tell me anything.

When I informed him that Michael had been stationed five hundred miles north of Bien Hoa, he began to talk about other units that had been hit that night by ARVN troops. Five months later, after we demanded an investigation of Michael's death, the sergeant, when questioned by the Defense Department, denied that he had discussed any other friendly fires.

I asked the sergeant how much time I had before the news of Michael's death would be released to the media. "Two hours," he said, "no more than two hours."

It was my turn to rage. In anger I demanded he give me at least six hours. I explained that we had one daughter in college out-of-state and another at the University of Iowa, and that I would not allow them to hear it first on television or radio.

"I'm sorry," he said with detachment, "but my orders from the Defense Department allow me only two hours."

As I approached the telephone, he stopped me. "What are you going to do?"

"I'm going to call Senator Harold Hughes in Washington. He can arrange to delay this announcement."

The sergeant relented and said he would see what he could do. The Defense Department did delay the message—they delayed it so long, in fact, that it became necessary for us to contact the local news media ourselves thirty-six hours later.

The priest discussed funeral arrangements. I made two important requests: a white funeral, which had become common, and vocal music. We expected John's senior class of one hundred from Don Bosco High School to attend. Father called several days later to tell me that he had to have special permission for a white funeral and that he was not going to make the request; he didn't approve of music at a funeral; and there wouldn't be room to seat John's class. We didn't feel our requests were out of line, but we realized he was in charge. We felt the animosity was the result of refusing a military funeral—Father was a twenty-year military retiree.

As the two men left the house and got into the military vehicle, our son John came out of the barn. He told me later that when he saw the car he'd wondered if he was in some sort of trouble with the draft board. He had registered the previous week after turning eighteen.

He opened the back door and walked into the landing. I stood at the top of the stairs and calmly said, "John, it's Michael. He's gone. He's dead."

This hulk of a young man, who was just under six feet tall and weighed more than two hundred pounds, slowly collapsed to the floor. I stood frozen as he got to his feet and went to his bedroom, closing the door behind him.

My mind raced. What do I do now? Whom must I notify? How was I going to reach our daughters and bring them home? I looked at my husband, still sobbing with his head in his arms, and realized that he couldn't help me.

I went back to my basement room, took out my book of telephone numbers, and started dialing. I called my sister Louise in Des Moines and asked her to send Mike, her son-in-law, to Kansas City to pick up Mary, our nineteen-year-old, at college. I phoned her school, Rockhurst College, and talked to the business manager, whom I knew because Michael had attended the same school, and asked him to prepare Mary for the ride home. Mary spent those heartbreaking hours waiting for her ride to arrive consoling the gentleman who brought her the sad news.

I called Leona, a close friend in La Porte City, and asked her to drive to Iowa City to tell our other daughter, Patricia, and bring her home. When she reached her rooming house, she learned Patricia was in Dubuque for the weekend, so she drove another two hours to pick her up. Patricia reacted in much the same manner as her father had. She was out of control for a long time, beating the walls and screaming, while her college friends stood by.

Next I called my youngest brother, Howard, an engineer with Alcoa in Pittsburgh. He had always been close to our family. This sensitive man had been a World War II radio operator on a B-29 and had never forgotten his war experiences. Returning from a bombing run on northern Japan, he had flown over the devastation of Hiroshima mere hours after its annihilation. When I told Howard the news he said nothing—just hung up with a moan. Because he lived alone, I called him three times that day until I was satisfied he was in control.

To reach my older brother in Lake City, Iowa, I called his bank and was told he was at the airport in Omaha. He had just put his wife on a plane to fly to Spokane, where their daughter was expecting her third child. Not long after, Bill returned my call and said he would drive to our farm immediately.

My youngest sister, Isobel Strathman, lived with her family in Pocahontas, Iowa. She, too, had had a distressful day on Thursday and had found solace in church, praying the rosary. It was she who had accompanied me to the hospital the morning Michael was born and had helped care for him the first six months of his life. She said they would come that afternoon.

I asked Father Robert Hirsch, superintendent of Don Bosco High School, to drive a short distance to Dewar, Iowa, to give the sad news to an eighty-year-old couple. These people had been friends of Gene's family for fifty years, and Michael had played the role of a grandson in their lives.

I made one final call to friends in La Porte City. The youngest of their four sons had been killed recently in Vietnam. Only a few short months before, I had tried to console the mother when they received the death message. She had turned on me in anger when I told her, "Your son died for his country." Later, I apologized to them for reopening wounds. They said with muffled voices, "Now someone in this community knows how we hurt."

While I was making my calls, Gene had gotten up from the table to console John. He found him lying flat on his bed; he looked up at his father and said, "Dad, Mike has it made, it's all over for him—he's in heaven." At this time Gene removed a locked fishing tackle box from the closet shelf. The last night at home Michael had told his father about it and asked him not to open it. Gene broke the lock, to find a long list of names and addresses: "The important people in my life." Pallbearers were chosen from this list.

A second note concerned his army life insurance, a $10,000 policy. He left $2,500 to his father, $2,500 to me, $2,500 to a student in his class when he taught in graduate school—a special request to enable the young woman to attend medical school—and the remaining $2,500 to Don Bosco High School to be spent on the purchase of lab equipment for the chemistry department. Michael's entire life had been organized, even to the end. Gene and I were saddened as we speculated on our son's state of mind when he wrote these final notes before leaving home.

Only when I had finished notifying the people closest to our family did I surrender to a rush of feelings—the crumbling of castles, the very destruction of our hopes, the loss of our brilliant twenty-five-year-old son.

At eighteen, his goal had been to find new foods to wipe out starvation throughout the world. While home for a weekend during his college days, he stood at our east living-room window overlooking a cornfield and remarked, "Mom, by the year 2000 starvation in the world will be so widespread we won't be able to use our corn and beans to fatten livestock." While in Vietnam, he had made plans to return to the University of Missouri at Columbia to complete his studies for a doctorate in biochemistry. Notice of his acceptance to the university had reached him one week before his death.

He had no desire to kill anything. His life and dreams were now gone, the result of one fatal mistake by his own artillery during a military action in a conflict that no one in power knew how to bring to an end.

# FOUR : THE HOMECOMING

During our nine-day wait for Michael's body, I made telephone calls to the Pentagon. I was often treated with insensitivity by military personnel and soon became irritated over their consistent failure to make good on promises. Now that I've had more than twenty years to reflect on that week's events, I realize that many of the demands I made represented firsts for men who seemed unable to make independent decisions or think on their feet. It was obviously not part of their training.

We were told by our service officer, Captain McDougal, that the body would be escorted home by a military man of our choosing and that he would return the next day to pick up the name of the person we selected. Referring to Michael's list of friends, we gave him the name of Tom Hurley, stationed at Bien Hoa. He'd been in Michael's chemistry class at Rockhurst. The Defense Department ignored our selection and wired us the name of a total stranger serving on a burial detail in the States.

We did not accept the Pentagon's choice and repeated our original request to Captain McDougal. It was granted only because it was demanded by Iowa Senator Harold Hughes, a powerful member of the Senate Armed Services Committee. Later, through correspondence from families who lost sons, we learned that rarely did they have an escort of their choice. Many families considered the offer of special escorts as just another military tactic, a salve to soothe the awful hurt when delivering the death message.

United Flight 210 approached the Waterloo airport and touched ground about 7:00 P.M., March 1, 1970. After discharging passengers and luggage at the main gate, it taxied slowly to a darkened corner of the airport. The aluminum casket containing Michael's remains was carefully removed and transferred to the awaiting hearse. Gene and Mary stood nearby, tearfully watching, accompanied by Tom Hurley's father and mother, who had driven up from Missouri to spend the few hours with their son. The casket was taken directly to the funeral home in Waterloo for the night, where it was opened by the undertaker. Gene and Mary viewed the body and confirmed that it was Michael's. He didn't appear to have a mark on him. I'd secretly hoped his body would show some damage, a testament that he'd died in war. It would have been easier to part with a ravaged body than give up a son who appeared to be asleep.

The decision to bring Michael home to the farm the next day was spontaneous, a manifestation of our Irish heritage. We wanted him with us, not abandoned in a mortuary. I sat alone on the davenport all night, neither praying nor thinking, wrapped in numbness. I wanted to prolong my last hours with my son, resting nearby. From time to time, John Staggs, his closest college friend, would appear with a cup of coffee, give me a hug, and then retreat to the kitchen. Sometime during the night Patricia dropped a sealed envelope into the casket. Gene came in to snip a lock of Michael's hair.

Morning came like any other morning on the farm, except for the neighbors. The women came to prepare breakfast, men to handle the

*Michael's high school graduation photo.*

chores. Family members dressed for the funeral. The undertaker fussed around the casket, arranging the mass of flowers, making room for the kneeling bench for our pastor's convenience.

Finally, it was nearing time for the last prayer and blessing before sealing the casket. As we gathered in the living room, I suddenly noticed that our priest was not there. It was hard enough being a Catholic family in a Protestant community. Now we had to endure an affront.

The problems with our priest had been endless since the day he came with the military officer to tell us of Michael's death. He visited us only once during the nine days of waiting—he failed to invite two former parish priests who were close to Michael to the funeral.

*A rubbing of Michael's name from the Vietnam Veterans Memorial in Washington, D.C.*

The Don Bosco teaching staff was ignored—our requests for music and a white funeral were denied. We were not surprised that he didn't come for the final prayers.

Paul Hochstetter, who had sold us Knights of Columbus insurance for our children, eventually came into the living room and whispered to me that he was a deacon in the church. Paul said the prayers.

With the help of faculty friends from Don Bosco, John's class came to the service at the church, and the school choir sang loud and clear. Our pastor accepted an invitation to dine with us after the service, but none of us ever saw him again. The casket was adorned with the flag, only because Michael's father insisted—I was ready to burn it. The church was packed to overflowing.

Michael was buried in the Mullen family plot in a country churchyard at Eagle Center, Iowa. To save space he was interred on top of the grave site of our second son, Daniel, born on May 22, 1947, who died on May 24. The boys are the fifth generation of Mullens to be buried there.

The Gold Stars customarily awarded to families of fallen soldiers were never presented to us. Gene might have refused them anyway—I didn't ask, and he didn't discuss it. The Pentagon officials with whom I dealt must have been asking each other, "Why isn't this woman behaving like a grieving mother's supposed to?"

The young soldier who escorted Michael's body to our home had been in Vietnam only a short time. After accompanying his friend's flag-draped casket to its final resting place, Tom had to return to the carnage. As we said our thanks and good-byes, he put his arms around me. "Please, Mrs. Mullen," he said, "don't give up. Protest this war."

A number of our Protestant friends sent cash memorials to us after Michael's funeral. In searching for an appropriate memorial, we decided on a scholarship in our parish for two students to attend the rural Catholic high school where our children had gone. Before finalizing this decision, we discussed our plan with the generous donors. However, Father didn't acknowledge our request, and the scholarships were not honored.

At one point during my wait for Michael's body, I had asked Captain McDougal if I could have the names of families who lost sons in the same friendly fire incident that killed my boy. We were told that such information was considered classified and would not be available to us. Almost four months later, however, a letter from a West Virginia mother reached our rural mailbox. She had heard from the army that we had wanted her to contact us, since her son died in the same incident. "We know now how everyone feels who had a son killed over there," she wrote. "It just isn't home here anymore." Even though she had seven other children, she told of how lonesome she felt after the death of her son. "I don't know what to write since I never wrote to you before," she concluded, "but I hope we can be good friends as our son and your son was."

This letter led to a friendship through the mail, and two years later while vacationing in the East we paid a visit to the family. The road to their farm was narrow and wound through the Appalachians. Our new friends were in the barn milking cows when we drove up, and it was several minutes before they ventured outside. They approached our car hesitantly—after all, we were strangers from another world.

We stayed for two days, soaking up the quiet. A calmness settled over us for the first time since Michael died. We sat on the porch swing of their weather-beaten home, getting acquainted and listening to the sounds of the mountains. Lulu missed her son—they'd spent many happy days tramping up and down the mountains hunting deer. She told of going out alone now that he was gone and how much it helped her bear the grief.

One afternoon our hosts asked if we would accompany them to their son's grave. We traveled a short distance up the mountain to a well-kept cemetery. The grave was covered with flowers, and it was obvious the mother was a regular visitor. As we looked around she pointed out three more Vietnam soldiers' graves, and I was reminded again of who was doing all the fighting and dying over there—the boys from the mountains, the ghettos, and the farms.

Gene and I returned to West Virginia in August 1974. We relaxed, ate too much, and laughed. We left the top of the mountain with hugs for everyone. As we headed south to Wheeling, West Virginia, we turned on the car radio. Against the peace of this setting, we suddenly heard Richard Nixon's farewell address. He was announcing his resignation as president.

Gene and I didn't utter a word. Our healing two-day vacation ended abruptly as my mind recalled the 30,000 men whose lives had been snuffed out during Nixon's tenure. The politician who had campaigned in 1968 to bring the boys home was leaving in disgrace after six years. I bitterly remembered his boastful statements when he referred to his support by the "silent majority." I thought of a January 1969 article on the back page of the *Des Moines Register* which quoted Secretary of State Henry Kissinger: "Mr. President, don't worry about the Vietnam War—put it on the back burner and I'll take care of it."

In the days immediately following Michael's funeral, I found myself consumed with a new purpose. I desperately needed a vehicle through which I could work out my grief, so I decided to help bring an end to the Vietnam War. It never occurred to me that an Iowa farmwife couldn't accomplish what had eluded three presidents.

Of course, the news media were available, always on the lookout for someone to speak out. They found in me a willing subject, and I made the most of my opportunities to be heard. A war-weary American public was now in the mood to listen, and as the letters poured in, I discovered a network of activists that stretched across the country.

Even if we had wanted to close the file on Michael's death, it would have been impossible to do so.

# FIVE : A SILENT MESSAGE

Several weeks after Michael's death we received a financial payment for his having given his life in the service of his country. The check represented six months' gratuity pay in the amount of $1844.40. It lay uncashed on our kitchen table for a while. At least once a day either Gene or I would say, "What'll we do with the damn thing?"

Gene was still working second shift at John Deere and got home after midnight. I always waited up for him to share an hour of intense conversation over coffee and a snack. I'm not sure whose idea it was to spend the check on an antiwar ad in the *Des Moines Register*, but the decision was reached early one morning in March of 1970.

Later, I called the *Register* and asked for the advertising manager. I described what we wanted to do and asked how much space we could have for $1844.40. He gave me half a page in a prime location, the bottom half of page three in the first section of the Sunday edition.

The next evening while discussing concepts for the ad, Gene came up with the idea of displaying a black cross for each Iowa boy who had died in Vietnam. To represent all the victims properly, we needed to ascertain whether any of them had been Jewish. I called a friend on the staff of the *Register* and asked him to research this dilemma and get us the actual count of the dead. He discovered that 114 more men from Iowa had lost their lives in Vietnam than had been included in the weekly totals released by the Pentagon. It had long been rumored that the death count was being deliberately juggled to conform to President Nixon's demand that no more than one hundred U.S. casualties be reported each week.

With the true count, I sat down to several hours of writing, tossing paper after paper into the wastebasket and drinking coffee. By the time Gene drove in from work that night I had put our ad together:

> A SILENT message to fathers and mothers of Iowa: We have been dying for nine, long, miserable years in Vietnam in an undeclared war . . . how many more lives do you wish to sacrifice because of your SILENCE? Sgt. Michael E. Mullen—killed by friendly fire.

And next, we placed a field of stark black crosses followed by another short message:

> These 714 crosses represent the 714 Iowans who have died in Vietnam In memoriam to Vietnam War Dead whom our son joined on February 18, 1970 . . . and to those awaiting the acceptable sacrifice in 1970 . . .
>
> Sponsored by Mr. and Mrs. Gene Mullen, La Porte City, Iowa

Our message appeared in the *Des Moines Sunday Register* on April 12, 1970. The response was overwhelming. We were contacted that day by practically every major newspaper in the United States and by several television networks. Many of the callers wanted to know what advertising agency had prepared the ad. They found it hard to believe that it had been the work of an Iowa farm couple. We

**A SILENT message to fathers and mothers of Iowa:**

**We have been dying for nine, long, miserable years in Vietnam in an undeclared war . . . how many more lives do you wish to sacrifice because of your**

**SILENCE?**

Sgt. Michael E. Mullen — killed by friendly fire

*These 714 crosses represent the 714 Iowans who have died in Vietnam

In memoriam to Vietnam War Dead whom our son joined on February 17, 1970 . . . and to those awaiting the acceptable sacrifice in 1970 . . .

Sponsored by Mr. and Mrs. Gene Mullen, La Porte City, Iowa

*Our Silent Message, which appeared as a half-page ad in the* Des Moines Register *on Sunday, April 12, 1970. The newspaper inadvertently used the wrong death date instead of the actual date of February 18. One hundred and thirty-eight Iowans died in Vietnam after this ad appeared.*

had hoped to appeal to the "silent majority," specifically to fathers and mothers, pleading for them to join us in our crusade for peace. They heard us, loud and clear. Letters filled our mailbox, some days in bundles.

"Dear Mr. and Mrs. Mullen," wrote James Hearst of Cedar Falls, Iowa, a foremost poet in the Midwest and a revered teacher at the University of Northern Iowa:

> Your silent message in the Sunday issue of the *Des Moines Register* made a deep impression on me. Its graphic expression gave a kind of dramatic release to the frustration and sense of injustice we find almost unbearable. Thank you for your courageous action. I shall put the "message" on my bulletin board for my students to see.

A father wrote that his son had been drafted out of graduate school:

> If we continue our present policy of intervention in all foreign conflicts . . . then in each generation, every mother's son must

face the possibility of death on the battlefield in wars which are totally unrelated to our own defense. . . .

Your message is very forcefully conveyed to those of us who have been silent.

Respectfully yours,
One of the silent majority

"I want to thank you in the name of all parents," wrote a man from Des Moines:

As the father of four sons that will be caught in the grist mill of this useless genocide, and as a man that served in both WW II and the police action in Korea, rest assured that I will join you in the vocal protest by every means that I can command. I have taken copies of your ad and placed them in the car windows, at my place of business and at home.

"We have a son who has been serving in Vietnam since the first of January," wrote parents from Hillsboro, Iowa. "We hope and pray each day that we don't receive a message such as you did. We won't remain silent any longer. Please include us in your plans. You have at least made some sort of start."

A couple from Clear Lake, Iowa, wrote:

Dear Mrs. Mullen:

Our son was lucky to come home in February. He told us the same things your son wrote to you. We have felt the same way about this war for a long time . . . and would be willing to help you in any campaign you think would focus attention on the war. It is being pushed more and more into the background and the public is becoming accustomed to it. Only the ones who have boys there or have been there seem to be interested.

Our son was pulled out in a troop withdrawal after being there 8 mo.—He has one year left in the service and now he has been assigned to go back for 8 more months. He did not volunteer! This our government don't tell! . . .

We are hoping the young people take to the streets again this next "Peace" day—April 15—That seems to be the only way they get any attention. . . .

From Illinois in April of 1970 a mother wrote:

Dear Mrs. Mullen:

Words cannot express the sympathy I have in my heart for you and your husband over the loss of your son.

I have been opposed to the Vietnam war and the draft for so long. I, too, joined the Silent Majority when our president so requested, to give him a chance to find a solution. But I feel we have been silent long enough. It's time the mothers unite.

A mother who had lost a son in Vietnam wrote:

Dear Mr. and Mrs. Mullen:

I wish to commend you on your action of placing an ad in an Iowa newspaper yesterday. I feel it was a courageous, a moral, a patriotic thing to do.

My son was killed in Vietnam Nov. 24. Thirty-nine more American boys were killed yesterday. What can we do? This country has elected two presidents by the democratic process because they promised to end or get us out of the war in Vietnam. We should never have gotten into it. And yet this country is still drafting and still killing young Americans there.

It is not necessary for me to say that the tragic, senseless death of a fine promising young son leaves scars that can never be erased.

One mother called on Sunday after reading our message in the paper and followed up with a letter. She had lost a son in Vietnam:

People tell me you have wonderful memories and this I realize, but the one tragedy surely overshadows all those memories, and I keep wondering why the good boys pay such a dear price. . . .

Since our son was killed I awaken at about 2:45 every morning and oh, Mrs. Mullen, how I ache. Only someone like you can understand. Sympathy is something I don't want, but wouldn't it be nice to have understanding.

We heard from one couple whose son had died in 1944 during World War II. In offering their condolences, they said that "the sorrow and loss remain for an eternity."

In April 1970 a mother in Iowa wrote that she would be sending copies of our ad to the president and to her representatives in Congress. Two of the crosses in our message represented the lost lives of two she knew well, she said. One of those boys planned to return and marry her daughter.

"My husband wrote such strong letters to our congressman that sometimes I expected they might send investigators to see us," wrote the mother of Michael's roommate his senior year at Rockhurst. Her son had been to Vietnam and back.

"I'm enclosing the $200.00 I promised," a Dr. Long wrote. "However on the basis of having lived in this old world for 60 years, spending most of that time attempting to figure out how things happen, and why we act as we do, I submit the following observations for whatever they may be worth." He wrote an entire page on how to go about a peace campaign, how to handle the press, and how to use available help so the load wouldn't overwhelm. He concluded:

> I have observed that any investigation of the war appears to die by the wayside or is white-washed. I speculate that pressure is applied somehow. It will be interesting to see if this pressure is applied to you.

On one occasion there was a dramatic change of heart. The Monday following Sunday's publication, I turned on Paul Harvey's noon radio show, which aired from WGN in Chicago. In the Chicago area it also appeared on local TV. The Silent Message ad was the backdrop on his program that day, and he announced that the message had done it to him. No longer would he be a "hawk" on the Vietnam War.

Then, there were families tormented beyond endurance. Their sons and brothers were gone—that's all they knew: "We have lived in a limbo of anguish for three and one-half years in our home waiting to hear if our son is alive or dead. I know how your heart hurts."

When mothers of POWs wrote, I found it difficult to respond but tried to persuade them to join all of us who were desperately trying to bring the conflict to an end. Only then would their sons come home.

Before long, I found myself despising everyone in military uniform. Letters from officers in the field, chaplains, and men in the Pentagon all incensed me. I couldn't understand how educated men, particularly men of God, could participate in a war without a purpose. Many of their letters duplicated each other. Phrases were rote; dates and signatures were rubber-stamped.

Soon real letters began to arrive—letters written from the heart, filled with compassion and love. But most of all they spoke the truth. These letters came from the grunts, the men who had fought the war—enlisted men, draftees, and friends and acquaintances of Michael's in Vietnam. When I suggested to the editor of the *Register* that Michael's letters home would make good reading, he was excited to get the material, and he printed them in full on Sunday, March 29, 1970. At that moment, it hadn't occurred to me that they would reach Michael's platoon in Vietnam. Their letters echoed the sentiments he voiced when writing to us. They were surprised to discover that their "straight" sergeant was writing the truth about the war.

Their letters contained different versions of the accident that killed Michael. Some of the men accepted their CO's contention that the artillery had been drinking. Others believed the gun was faulty. Many, however, didn't believe anything they were told.

When the first man from the unit who returned stateside paid us a visit, we learned that sixty GIs had signed a letter to us in which they'd asked for help and complained about conditions with the 198th, then under the command of Colonel Norman Schwarzkopf. The letter had been intercepted, and the soldiers were threatened with court-martial if they continued to correspond with the Mullens. Somehow, we'd become the enemy.

One young soldier, M.L.C., defied the threat and continued to correspond in hopes of being pulled out of combat. It paid off—he spent the final months of his tour in comparative safety as a clerk in the Americal headquarters in Chu Lai. There, he learned firsthand about body count and other means employed by officers to assure advancement following their six-month tour.

Before he transferred out of the field, he wrote us this warning:

Dear Mrs. Mullen:

Today we're informed of rights in the army. If any people write to you, their future is in jeopardy if you publish any of the mail. For they can be court-martialed for mutiny and undermining the army. Don't publish any articles because it could bring harm to people and their future. If there are any questions you want answered—have the congressman write and ask them. He can register them and no one can be prosecuted. The people here would like a copy of any letter sent you from here.

Anything sent to you can be censored as we are in a war zone. So please have your congressman ask the questions.

Sincerely,
M.L.C.

This letter had been opened and words blacked out. It was the only one from Vietnam that had been censored, although mail continued to reach us from all over the war zone.

Gene and I became more and more interested in locating Colonel Schwarzkopf. We wanted to hear his version of what happened the night Michael was killed. Eventually, we learned that the colonel was in the D.C. area, so during a trip to the capital in late summer of 1971, we visited him at Walter Reed Army Hospital. We found him confined to a hospital bed in a full body cast, after surgery for a spinal injury. When I asked if his hospitalization was connected to his service in the war, he smiled and replied, "Hell, no! This was the result of an old football injury while playing too many years of football at West Point." Nineteen years later we read in the September 10, 1990, issue of *Newsweek* a story of the medals Schwarzkopf earned for "wounds received in Vietnam (not including the spinal surgery he needed to repair the damage done by parachuting)."

Gene and the colonel talked at length about the night Michael was killed. Schwarzkopf described how angry he'd been when he learned of the accident and noticed a pile of empty beer cans near the guns. The colonel told Gene he'd wanted to kill the artillery CO; he added that his men were not allowed to drink beer while on a mission. (Declassified material that I later received from the investigation of the incident stated that the beer cans were not relevant to the issue.)

After we left the hospital, I went to a public pay telephone and dialed Colonel Pogoloff, the former artillery CO, at his home. I told him who I was and accused him of allowing his men to drink beer on duty. Colonel Pogoloff became hostile: "Did Schwarzkopf tell you that? Well, I'll take care of Norm one of these days."

We continued to hear stories of the 198th, and I remember one that none of the men in Charlie Company forgot. They were to have a stand-down, a three-day rest at base headquarters, in January 1970. When they arrived back at Chu Lai, they found their beer locked up until two o'clock in the afternoon. They'd sent money back to the base to be sure it would be iced and waiting for them. Expecting to relax, they were ordered instead to police the base and clean up litter scattered by the regular army stationed there. This abuse poured upon men who had come into base after sixty days of tramping through the muck of the jungle. To top it off, the GIs later had to sit on bleachers in the hot sun while the commanding officer lectured them on the art of jungle warfare. These men had lived jungle warfare twenty-four hours a day for the past two months. If they needed a lecture, it should've addressed how to survive a tour of duty with the Americal Division.

When I heard about the harassment endured by Charlie Company, I wanted an explanation from the battalion commander. I wrote to Schwarzkopf in mid April and soon received his response. His letter noted that most of the time stand-downs were used to provide soldiers an opportunity to relax. Training activities during stand-downs, however, were also necessary in order to maintain the soldiers' skills. Because of the high rate of turnover due to the one-year tour of duty in Vietnam, his letter stated, these training activities were especially important. The letter was signed, "Sincerely, H. Norman Schwarzkoff."

I noticed that he didn't mention turnover due to death and injury. At the time, I believed the colonel had actually written and signed the letter himself. Now I am amused to note that his name was misspelled. After reading it, I understood my son's frustration and anger—I only wondered why the man's entire unit hadn't rebelled.

Years later we got a phone call from a man who identified himself as former Captain Robert Duguid, the chaplain who was on the ground with Michael's company the night he was killed. He said he was in the Midwest on vacation and wanted to visit us. We were pleased to welcome anyone who had been with Michael in the service, so we urged him to stop by. As we waited for him we recalled Charlie Company's stories about the chaplain. He'd been considered a bad omen, and the men were always unhappy when he accompanied them on a mission. It seemed that something never failed to go wrong when he was along.

He arrived several hours later, another veteran who hadn't

exorcised the demons of Vietnam. He paced our living-room floor and described the experience of strapping on a holster and gun to accompany the colonel into the jungle to shoot "gooks." I cringed when he described the enemy as "gooks"—a derogatory term used by the grunt in the field. My opinion of the Vietnam army chaplain dropped several notches. At one point Gene interrupted him to ask if he was familiar with the International Code of War, which prohibited chaplains from bearing arms. He ignored the question.

We'd looked forward to his visit, but he left us outraged. He didn't resemble padres we'd met in World War II, but he certainly fit the image of an Americal officer. I have occasionally felt remorse over some of the bitter letters I wrote following Michael's death, but never the ones I wrote to the chaplain.

When Michael was leaving for Vietnam, I told him that if he was assigned to the Americal Division, I didn't want to know about it. Unfortunately, when his first letter arrived home, it bore the return, "The Americal Division, 198th." We'd discussed the Americal even before Michael was drafted in 1968. One of his high school classmates had returned from Vietnam and had described his experiences serving in the infamous division. Initially made up of a thousand men, Americal had been sent into combat in 1967. All members of this troubled unit were educated, ranging from junior college credits to doctorate degrees, and all had refused to undergo officer's training. In spite of their intelligence, their casualty rate was enormous; more than two-thirds of the original one thousand men were either killed or wounded.

The Americal was plagued with problems throughout its campaign in I Corps, the northernmost of four military sectors in Vietnam. My aversion to this division and fear for Michael's safety within it grew daily. I continued to read everything I could about the unit. By late November, we were beginning to get reports of an incident at My Lai, a hamlet located in the area under the Americal command. A platoon under the leadership of a young lieutenant had actually wiped out an entire hamlet—men, women, and children. The massive killing of these Vietnamese occurred in March 1968, but the Americal headquarters managed to cover up the incident, and it didn't reach the news media until the fall of 1969. I clipped the newspaper item and enclosed it with my next letter to Michael. He wrote back: "You've got to remember this is an area that is strongly

VC and even today the 11th Division operating there is constantly running into booby traps, etc. You will find that the thing was ballooned all out of proportion as to what actually happened."

I didn't agree with him. I felt the troops in I Corps were being told something other than what we were getting from the media at home. I'd read a former Americal colonel's characterization of the men under his command as "dumb dogfaces." The first Americal troops sent to Vietnam were probably better educated than most of the officers. Combat duty in the jungle was an ordeal for everyone, but it must have been particularly irritating for the men to be taking orders from officers like the colonel.

In another letter Michael had made a passing reference to the Americal's officers' preoccupation with body count. "Have to laugh at them," he said, "for they live in a dream world. They have to have figures (body count) and nobody knows what is a VC or a plain ignorant villager, at least in this area."

Shortly after its deployment, the Americal had adopted as its basic tactic a refined search-and-destroy method known informally as the scorched-earth policy. Michael's letter of October 22, 1969, described burning two villages during one of the search-and-destroy missions the president had promised to discontinue.

That same year *Esquire* published a story by Robert A. Gross about following orders in Vietnam. In it a young soldier talked about his experience. "I was 21," he said. "I was really scared." He went on to say that he had eased himself into the use of torture: "It took a while to get used to using brutality; you didn't know what the effects would be. I didn't particularly like the idea of torture but I wasn't going to prevent it. I preferred the friendly approach of giving prisoners cigarettes to gain their friendship. Whether or not I got brutal depended on how cooperative they were. But I don't think I was sadistic at all."

He admitted to having used clubs, rifle butts, pistols, and knives on prisoners interrogated at Hill 28, base camp of the 1st Battalion of the 1st Cavalry, Americal Division. He said his captain told him he could use "any technique I could think of" but cautioned against beating prisoners in the presence of outsiders, "like a visiting officer or perhaps the Red Cross."

The soldier saw ARVN personnel kicking a prisoner to death and tried in vain to stop them. After the man died, the Americal captain had him placed in two five-hundred-pound rice sacks and taken into the jungle to be dumped. The victim was then added to the body count.

Immediately after the publication of Michael's letters, I heard from an Iowa woman whose oldest son, also named Michael, had been drafted out of college and was now serving with the Americal Division at Chu Lai. "Your son's letters could almost be ours," she said. "My husband read excerpts from each, and you could say they were close to the same place at the same date. Very close."

We received another letter from her three months later. Bringing us up-to-date, she told us her Mike had taken R and R in Hawaii, then returned to Chu Lai, where he went out on patrol almost immediately. Shortly afterward, the family had received a phone call:

> Mike was in a hospital in Japan, hurt but alive. His words to us were, "My part of this God-forsaken war is over! I'm coming home." He wouldn't talk about what happened, but said his parts were all still with him, that he was burned. He had been told that we had been notified, but we hadn't been.
>
> It seems to me that the boys from the Americal are taking hell these last several months, and it's hard to think of these beautiful young men sacrificing so much for a cause they virtually despise.

A Massachusetts veteran who had served with the 196th Light Infantry Brigade in Vietnam contacted us in 1978 after reading *Friendly Fire.* He said the book's account of Michael's death led him to believe that this was very common in the Americal Division. During his tour of duty, he wrote, there had been numerous instances of GIs being killed in a similar fashion. He recounted an incident on February 2, 1968, when eight men were killed and fourteen wounded in his platoon when they were mortared by a company from the 198th. It was common knowledge, he said, that the 198th was as dangerous as the North Vietnamese army.

Our government had waged war in I Corps for almost five years, suffering horrendous losses in combat and an inordinate number of deaths by friendly fire. They had gained no territory in all those years. On April 30, 1970, I wrote the following to Frank Reynolds of ABC following an evening broadcast that upset me.

Dear Mr. Reynolds:

On your news this evening you told the American public that 94 young men had died in combat in Vietnam last week. Why can't you tell us in honest figures how many really died in Vietnam last week?

As the mother of a young man who died on a night defensive ambush, who is not considered a war casualty because he was killed by friendly fire, I find it most difficult each Thursday evening to swallow the figure put out by the Pentagon. Many of us believe one-third who die each week are not reported on the weekly toll.

Just had to be heard!

Sincerely,
Peg Mullen

# SIX : THE MARINES

The spring after Michael's death, I became fascinated with a series of articles in the *Des Moines Register* about five marines who were facing court-martial in I Corps. According to the *Register,* these men had been on patrol the night of February 18, had been fired on, and had returned fire. The next day a number of dead villagers were found, among them women and children.

Our son had been killed February 18. We originally had been told by our service officer that his death was by action of the ARVN—one of five similar ambushes that night.

The newspaper listed the marines' names and their home towns. I decided to try to reach each family and forward copies of the stories I'd clipped.

On April 12, 1970, I wrote to these families, simply addressing each, "To family of [marine's name], city and state." I added a notation to each envelope asking the Postal Service to please deliver, as this young man was in trouble in Vietnam and I had important information for his family. At this time, I was receiving mail with little more address than "Peg, Iowa," so I had faith that the letters would somehow be delivered.

Dear :

On February 21 we received word from the Army that our son was killed while on a night defensive ambush, the result of friendly artillery fire.

We demanded to know from the military officer what was meant by "friendly fire." He told us our son was killed by fire from the South Vietnamese Army and that it was not accidental. He then proceeded to tell us that our son was a victim of one of five deliberate shellings in Vietnam on February 18 by the South Vietnamese. He explained that the ARVN had been infiltrated by the Vietcong. In checking back through the newspapers we find that there was a deliberate shelling at Bien Hoa that night. Then on a late news program on the radio Sunday, February 22, we heard of a Marine unit near Danang that was attacked by a unit of the ARVN and in the return fire the five Marines killed Vietnamese civilians and were confined to the brig.

We intend to pursue an investigation of our son's death through the office of Senator Harold Hughes, and we are wondering if you would care to tell us the outcome of your son's story. If you decide not to correspond, we'll understand.

Sincerely,
Peg Mullen

The first response came by telephone. Mrs. James Schwarz of Weirton, West Virginia, near Pittsburgh, was an angry woman, refusing to believe that her decorated marine son was in trouble. She and her family were strong backers of the military, raised the flag every day, and were proud of their marine.

Mrs. Schwarz followed up her call with a letter on April 23, offering us her deepest sympathy on the death of our son "in this senseless, useless war." She had received only two letters from her son. He told of being on a night patrol when they were fired upon by a small child. All but five of their patrol were killed, and the survivors were ordered to return fire.

After the family received the second letter, they were unable to find out anything more about what was going on. Even though the local marine officer in Pittsburgh denied it, Mrs. Schwarz was convinced that her son was not receiving their letters, nor were his being delivered to her or to his wife. She suspected that the military feared his letters might reveal what was really going on. She closed by asking me to let her know if I found out anything about what happened that night, and she offered to help in any way she could.

Mrs. Schwarz sent along copies of letters that had come to her and her daughter-in-law (Micheal Schwarz's wife) from officers in the marine command in Vietnam. The first, addressed to the marine's wife, came from Schwarz's company commander, First Lieutenant L. R. Ambort. He provided the family with an account of what happened during the night of February 19, 1970. He told Mrs. Schwarz that her husband had volunteered for a five-man night combat patrol. Shortly after the patrol left their night defensive position they were hit by enemy fire, and they returned fire.

He went on to say that the next day a friendly patrol found the bodies of sixteen women and children in the area where Schwarz's patrol had made enemy contact the night before. He told of a preliminary investigation being held, which was followed by the arrest of the five marines. Pretrial investigations were under way to determine if court-martials would be filed. Lieutenant Ambort expressed his own opinion, standing behind the five young men, declaring them innocent, and assuring the family their son and husband would have adequate legal defense.

Another letter addressed to the parents came from Captain Daniel H. LeGear, a lawyer with the 1st Marine Division who was appointed to represent Micheal Schwarz. LeGear introduced himself and promised to do all he could to help their son.

Mrs. Schwarz had complained that, after receiving his first letter, she wrote to LeGear ten times before he answered. When he finally did, he assured her that he was doing everything he could to assist her Mike. He told of being in the middle of a formal investigation and added that he expected the case to be referred to a general court martial, alleging some form of unlawful killing. He suggested that the family obtain character statements in Mike's behalf, and with his letter he enclosed guidelines for obtaining suitable statements and asked that they be sent directly to him.

I wrote to Mrs. Schwarz again on April 27, after I had been in touch with another of the marines' families, the Joseph Krichtens of Hanover, Pennsylvania. This letter represented an attempt on my part to bring these families together.

La Porte City, Iowa
April 27, 1970
Dear Mrs. Schwarz:

We received your letter today. Now, I will tell you what I have read and learned by writing letters. Our boy was killed on February 18 about 2 A.M. while on a night defensive ambush near Tam Ky, between Chu Lai and Danang. At that time we were told by the military serviceman who came to our house that five units of Americans had been attacked at that time by the South Vietnamese. We were interested in reading the story about your boy because it happened at about the same time and in the same area.

There were two stories in our *Des Moines Register* concerning it, and two radio stories. We don't know the name of the station because it was something my son John and a friend of his heard late at night. The stories were along the theme that the Marines had been attacked by the South Vietnamese who were patrolling with them. However, I didn't hear the broadcasts so can't give you the facts.

When I wrote to the families of the five Marines whose names were listed in the *Des Moines Register*, I prayed they'd respond. On April 26, I heard from Mrs. Joseph E. Krichten, 419 Third St., Hanover, Pennsylvania, and I think she would be close enough for you to contact in person. She gave me the address of Mrs. William Boyd, 109 Mary St., Evansville, Indiana. I've located families of three of the five Marines involved. The other boys listed were Randell Herrod, Calvin, Oklahoma, and Samuel Green, Cleveland. We still might hear from Oklahoma, but our letter to Cleveland came back for lack of address. If you know anyone in Cleveland, they might be able to locate Mrs. Green for you.

On April 26 I sent Mrs. Krichten in Hanover the two clippings from our paper so you can contact her to get copies.

I'm enclosing a copy of Mrs. Krichten's letter, and if I were you, I would suggest that you go to a leading newspaper in Pittsburgh and tell them your story. You simply have to have help from the public.

Please let me hear from you.

Sincerely,
Peg Mullen

When I heard from Mrs. Schwarz again, she expressed frustration over her dealings with the government and the news media. One Pittsburgh newspaper told her that they would not have anything to do with her son's case, and a local television station was not allowed even to discuss it. Only her local newspaper offered to help, saying they would contact Senator Robert Byrd of West Virginia.

Mrs. Schwarz sent us the responses she had gotten from Senator Hugh Scott of Pennsylvania, which she did not find very helpful, and she said it was clear that she would not hear from him again. She enclosed a list of the people she had written to without receiving replies: Senator Byrd of West Virginia, Senator Morgan of West Virginia, and Senator Schweiker of Pennsylvania. She'd written four letters to President Nixon.

Mrs. Schwarz had heard from Mrs. Krichten, who was not getting any more help than she was. She had also contacted her sister, a nun in Cleveland, to try to find the address of Mrs. Green. She let us know that she would stay in touch.

On May 6, 1970, I had a tearful call from Mrs. Schwarz. She had received a letter from her son's commanding officer. He was trying to get the boys out of the brig and return them to their company until time for their trials. She was frightened—actually afraid that her son would be shot in the back by his own troops. The call prompted me to write to the five families once again. By this time, I had obtained home addresses of all the marines. I wanted to tell them about Mrs. Schwarz's fear and give everyone involved the complete list of addresses:

La Porte City, Iowa
May 9, 1970
Dear friends:

Because I keep stumbling on news concerning your sons, I have more information to give you.

By making a call to the newspaper in Calvin, Oklahoma, I was able to learn that the grandfather of Randell Herrod had already made a trip to Vietnam in behalf of his grandson. The rest of you might want to contact him in an effort to learn what was the outcome. I called the *Plain Dealer* newspaper in Cleveland and found a reporter who had much information on Samuel Green.

He is mailing all the material that was printed in their paper, and he also gave me the home address of the boy.

When I called the home of Randell Herrod I learned his grandfather, Alvin Self, was not home. I talked to Randell's teenage brother and he told me their grandfather had been in Vietnam.

I would suggest that all of you together could get some help in Washington. I feel Mrs. Schwarz has a real reason to fear the fact that their last letter from Vietnam said an effort was being made to return the boys to duty before their trial. If their commanding officer is the man who preferred charges, I know that I couldn't leave a thing unturned at this point to save them from returning to duty in the same command.

When information comes from the reporter in Cleveland, I shall send it on to you.

Sincerely,
Peg Mullen

On June 23, the day after I learned Micheal Schwarz had been sentenced to life imprisonment, I wrote to Senator Hugh Scott. He remained one of the strongest supporters of the Vietnam War right up to the bitter end. I alluded to a visit made to his office earlier in the month in which I had discussed, with the senator's aide, the marines' situation and the coincidental death of my son.

I advised Senator Scott that, although one of the young men was a Pennsylvania resident and another lived just across the border, their story had not been covered by radio, television, or newspapers in that state. Tom Boyd, Randell Herrod, and Sam Green, I wrote:

were financially able to obtain civilian legal counsel, and all three had extensive aid from their congressmen and senators. Only Mrs. Krichten and Mrs. Schwarz had no money to get civilian counsel, and only these two were refused help from their government representatives.

Michael Krichten was given immunity because he said things the Marine Corps wanted him to say. Micheal Schwarz was made an example for all to see—he received a life sentence. Tom Boyd was acquitted today, because he had an attorney from Evansville,

Ind., who came to his defense. Sam Green and Randell Herrod should stand a chance as they have civilian defense attorneys.

In closing, I told Senator Scott that I understood the bitterness Mrs. Schwarz felt over her son's life sentence. "I, too, believe that the great, massive structure called the Pentagon has made a mockery of the flag and uniform," I said. "I also believe there will be a special hell for the men who have driven our boys in uniform in Vietnam to their deaths and disgrace, all in the name of patriotism."

On the same day, June 23, I wrote to Mrs. Schwarz:

> After visiting with you on Monday I was left with the awesome thought that no one cares anymore; that the poor have no place to turn for help as far as our government is concerned; that our government with its president is concerned only with war and kill . . . kill . . . kill. Our young sons and their futures have no meaning—we are to continue to breed boy babies just to keep the war machine functioning.
>
> Monday evening I drove about 40 miles to visit a widow who was to bury her handsome 23-year-old son. He had the great honor of being the first Iowan to die in Cambodia. I was frightened to find that she, too, felt the Pentagon had made a mockery out of the flag and patriotism. She was ready to kill anyone in uniform who approached her home—no flag will ever fly again at this home.
>
> After I talked to you, I called Mr. Stipe in Oklahoma, the attorney who is representing Randell Herrod. His secretary told me he had gone to Danang to defend Randy and would sit in on remaining trials as "friend of court." She said she'd have him call me or write when he returned. She felt the whole thing was a frame-up and wasn't sure how the rest of the trials would go—then today we hear that Tom Boyd was acquitted.
>
> I'm giving you Stipe's telephone number and if you don't feel like talking to him have someone else call for you. He is a kind man and I'm sure he has Micheal's interest at heart, in light of the fact he did make the trip to Danang to be there for his trial.
>
> I was so glad to hear that you had gone on TV, letting your anger show through. I didn't see it but my daughter did and called me. Don't give up—tell your Mike there are millions who do care.
>
> Sincerely,
> Peg Mullen

The same day I had a call from a friend in Pittsburgh who suggested that I tune in ABC News that evening. I did so and watched the Schwarz family set fire to the flagpole and flag. This action in 1970 didn't seem to disturb the president or the Congress.

In late July 1970 two Pittsburgh attorneys announced that they had enough evidence for an appeal on behalf of Micheal Schwarz. About the middle of December, attorney James McLaughlin was notified that Major General C. F. Widdecke, commanding general of the 1st Marine Division, had ordered the sentence reduced. The sentence was commuted from life to a dishonorable discharge and one year at hard labor. In his ruling the major general stated: "The great inconsistency is the fact Schwarz's platoon leader, who gave the order which Schwarz followed, was acquitted and is now attending college." Schwarz's attorney said he would continue to seek full exoneration for the marine.

Micheal's one-year sentence, which he served at the Portsmouth Naval Disciplinary Command prison, was reduced by seventy-seven days for good conduct. His attorney announced that another appeal on new evidence would be filed.

My last letter from Mrs. Schwarz came during the 1970 Christmas season, and it contained no good news. She opened with an apology for not having written sooner and then informed me that she had just brought her husband home from the hospital following a complete nervous breakdown. She described her trip to visit her son, whom she was able to see for less than an hour after a trip of five days. His wife and baby did not accompany her because the baby was sick. But Mrs. Schwarz thought this may have been just as well, since the time spent with her son was so short. In fact, she feared her visit made it even worse for her son.

The lawyer had promised that her son would be home for Christmas. Since he was not, they were still waiting to celebrate the holidays. Mrs. Green had phoned her at 4 A.M. on Christmas day, because she also had been promised that her son would be home in time for Christmas. This letter marked the first time Mrs. Schwarz addressed me as Peg and signed her letter with Helen.

Another of my original five letters was sent to the family of Thomas R. Boyd of Evansville, Indiana. The letter was not returned, nor was it answered. Several weeks later, Helen Schwarz informed me that she'd managed to get Boyd's address from the marine headquarters in Pittsburgh. I then wrote to Boyd's mother. Once again, there was no reply.

On May 1, 1970, I phoned Mrs. Boyd. She told me the family had hired an attorney who was planning to go to Vietnam along with investigators from Washington, D.C. She also said their family had obtained thousands of signatures from their area on petitions in support of Thomas.

On May 8 I called her again to relay the information Mrs. Schwarz had given me about their son's commanding officer. He had tried to have the five marines put back on duty with the platoon, pending their trials. Mrs. Boyd thanked me for the information and said she would pass it on immediately to her attorney.

According to accounts in the *Des Moines Register*, Boyd's trial followed that of Micheal Schwarz. His civilian attorney sat in with the military attorney, and they petitioned the court for trial by military judge and not by a full court-martial. This petition was granted. Boyd was found not guilty. He had testified in his own defense, telling the judge that, before he went to Vietnam, his pastor reminded him that one of life's most important rules was "Thou shalt not kill." Members of his platoon testified that they had never seen him kill anyone in combat.

As he left the courtroom, tears were streaming down his face. Private Samuel Green, himself awaiting trial, threw his arms around Boyd and his attorney.

The fourth letter, addressed to Green's family in Cleveland, was the only one to be returned. It had been incorrectly addressed. (I sent it without house number or street name.)

I had no luck in tracing the Green family, so I called the Cleveland paper and located a reporter who was familiar with the story. He promised to send me an item on the marine, together with Mrs. Green's address. The reporter, Dick Feager, followed through and sent me an article he had written on June 5, 1970, under the heading, "City Marine Accused of Killing in War Sues the U.S. Military."

Green's attorney, James Chiara, took an unusual approach in the defense of his client. He hired a Washington-based law firm and filed suit in federal court in the capital. The theme of his defense challenged the courts to rule on: "When a soldier kills, when is it duty and when is it murder?" His suit also asked that the court-martial be dropped, that Green be released from the stockade, that he be reinstated in the Marine Corps, and that all charges of wrongdoing be thrown out. During an interview with the press Chiara said: "The Vietnam War is a screwy war. It isn't fought to claim land. It is fought to kill people."

The attorney contended that Green was merely doing his duty—he was assigned to a "killer team" and sent out to kill. This incident followed closely the disclosure of the My Lai rampage, and our military was in no position to sweep this one under the rug.

In closed hearings before Green was formally charged, officers in the unit told of Vietnamese women and children serving in combat—reminding the judge that the night before all but five of the unit had been killed by ambush and that the survivors were sent out to "get some of the bastards." Talking to the press, Green's mother remarked: "My son didn't leave the country to get thrown into the pen. No wonder those boys don't want to go into service if they can't defend themselves."

After receiving Mrs. Green's address and telephone number, I called her and told her what I knew about the other families. I found her in the same emotional state as the other mothers: angry and confused about the military's role in Vietnam. She was eager to tell me that Representative Carl Stokes, from her district, was being helpful and that the family had hired a good attorney who planned to sit in on the trial in Danang with the marine counsel.

On August 15 and 16 the newspapers reported that Samuel Green had been found guilty of premeditated murder and sentenced to five years' imprisonment. One unnamed member of the "killer team" had testified during the one-day trial that he had not seen Green kill anyone, and the government's witness, Michael Krichten, also testified that he had not seen Green kill the Vietnamese. After the trial, Green commented that his automatic appeal probably would get him off.

The story of Randell Herrod, the fifth marine indicted for murder in Danang, had a sudden and happy ending. My letter of April 12 to the young man's family had been delivered.

After contacting the families of the other four, I decided to call the newspaper in Calvin, Oklahoma. The editor gave me the name of Alvin Self, the grandfather who had reared the boy, together with his address and telephone number.

I put in a call for Mr. Self and talked to a teenage brother of Private Herrod. He said their grandfather was in Vietnam. I became intrigued with this elderly gentleman from a rural community of 350 people who had actually gone to Vietnam.

On May 22, 1970, I had a call from Gene Stipe, a practicing attorney in McAlester, Oklahoma. He represented the family of Randy Herrod. He told me that Mr. Self had come to his office that day with a letter from me, which he found waiting for him on his return from Vietnam. Stipe asked where I had gotten my information and would I please send him everything I had in my possession.

The following day I mailed the attorney the materials he had requested, together with a letter asking that he return some of the documents, as they were originals. I also told him of my contacts with the marines' families thus far.

Two months later the *Des Moines Register* carried a story about Gene Stipe going to Vietnam in defense of Randell Herrod. He'd attempted to challenge the U.S. Court of Military Appeals, asking that Herrod be granted a change of venue and postponement of his trial on charges of premeditated murder. Herrod's marine lawyers had also challenged the court-martial system. These challenges were denied.

There were no developments in this case for weeks. On August 31, while entertaining guests from New York City, we heard a news bulletin over the radio announcing that Herrod had been acquitted. The news items coming from the press on the scene in Vietnam told that when Herrod heard the verdict, he picked up his military defense counsel and carried him bodily from the courtroom. Next he strapped on a pistol to escort attorney Stipe to the airport for his return to Oklahoma.

Herrod, who prior to this incident had been scheduled to receive the Silver Star for heroism in action, remarked that he had been prepared for the worst—the maximum penalty could have been death. His trial for murder, with the life or death of a young marine hanging in the balance, had lasted a single ten-hour day, and the jury was out for a scant three hours. Military justice is swift if not always fair.

# SEVEN : WBZ

In the months following my son's death, I refused to sign a blank pay voucher for his last eighteen days in Vietnam. When the service officer, Captain McDougal, came to me with the blank voucher, I told him I wouldn't sign it until the amount of pay earned was shown. He looked at me in disgust and replied that I was probably the first mother (or father) during all the years of the war to refuse. My refusal to sign the voucher was neither extraordinary nor symbolic, merely good business. Yet it seemed to upset nearly everyone in the military, from the general at Fort Benjamin Harrison (finance center for the U.S. Army) to our young service officer at the local level.

Eventually I was given the figures the army had calculated, but they did not agree with the figures Michael had sent home each month. He would send me his pay voucher, covered with notations—asking me to become familiar with the form and to keep them in my files. He seemed obsessed with the fear that the army would make money off of his service. The pay offered was less than $100 for eighteen days, and my records indicated his basic pay was $254.70 minus deductions of a saving bond and a $60 allotment.

Finally, I asked for an audit, making my request to a colonel in the Army Finance Center. He asked me to explain what I meant by an audit. I told him that I was not a certified public accountant nor was I an officer in the finance division of the army, but I certainly could explain an audit to him. The requested information came in the mail several days later, and I learned that the discrepancy was due to Michael's being charged for eleven days of unearned leave, eleven days of salary, eleven days of food and clothing rations, and eleven days of Social Security, including the Social Security paid by the Pentagon.

Despite many telephone conversations between the officers and me, the matter went unresolved. At one point they gave Michael a promotion in rank, but I refused to accept the compensation they offered. After months of wrangling, I concluded that the Defense Department needed the money worse than I did.

My anger peaked when I learned that, had Michael survived Vietnam and returned home, all of his unpaid leave would have been forgiven. When I thought of the millions of dollars flowing into Pentagon coffers from this operation, I became enraged. Efforts in the Senate in 1970 to repeal that provision of the law were unsuccessful, so it is still on the books.

I received a letter written on November 21, 1970, from a woman in Wisconsin. She was disturbed because her son had been wounded in Vietnam; then the death notice came labeling his death as nonhostile. She was engaged in a struggle with the Pentagon and Congress to learn the truth. The story of my battle with the Army Finance Center had been featured in the *Des Moines Register*. She wanted to tell me that her son had also paid back excess leave of 27½ days, explaining that the double FICA deduction was tax that Michael would have paid and also that portion paid by the government. She went on to remark that the army was very thorough in getting every cent from the ones who died, wondering why they didn't save lives as efficiently as they saved pennies.

For the Pentagon to collect for 27½ days of excess leave, it would have to be paid by the family unless the deceased had extra monies on hand in the military. I observed this situation repeatedly over the years, and I'm still at a loss to understand why any parent should be subjected to such an indignity when his or her family has already made the supreme sacrifice.

From the moment we buried Michael our correspondence with the Defense Department, in their effort to answer our questions, continued to amaze us. Contrary to mail coming from division officers in Vietnam—all written by one officer but signed by various officers—the mail from the Pentagon was not coordinated. Each department head expressed his own theory, with little regard to what the man next door was telling us.

We were determined to tell the world what we already knew. So when a call came late one afternoon in June of 1970 from Jerry Williams, who hosted a radio talk show from station WBZ in Boston, I readily accepted his invitation to join a panel of four women who were opposed to the Vietnam War. The show would air that night from eight to midnight. One of the panelists had asked him to contact me. I reminded him that I lived on a farm and that our telephone was a party line, shared by four households. I agreed to contact my neighbors. If it was OK with them, I would visit with his panel and callers from ten to midnight.

It was a stimulating two hours, with calls coming from many sections of the East. I welcomed this first opportunity to send my message beyond the Midwest. Williams also arranged for me to talk with the panelists, four women who would eventually form the nucleus of a powerful peace organization in Boston and throughout the state. At one point during the program I was asked what the women could do about the situation in Vietnam.

"March," I replied.

Jerry Williams hosted the oldest talk show on radio, and it covered the entire East Coast from Florida into Canada. I could hardly comprehend the territory I had reached—the numbers of people who had listened to my message. Were minds changed?

The only letters I received as a result of my participation came from the panelists themselves. One of them, Shirlie Goldman, proved to be a prolific correspondent. In her first letter, written the morning after the program, she said the panelists had agreed there should be a Mother's March on Washington sometime in the very near future. "We are beginning to make our plans, and I will keep you informed," she promised.

A hastily scrawled postcard dated June 9 arrived in the mail:

> *The Evening Star*
> Washington, D.C.
> Dear Peg:
> Right on, dear girl. A lot of people think your idea about the women marching is the last best hope.
> Shalom,
> Mary McGrory

True to her word, Shirlie kept me informed of their every activity. Within a few weeks of the broadcast, they had organized a march. "I thought you might be interested in our plans," she said in a June 27 letter:

> If you know any ladies in Iowa who would like to join us, please pass on the information. Even five would be great!
>
> Perhaps we'll get some publicity. Most of us were formerly the "Silent Majority," and we hope this will be an important wedge for "Silent Mothers" in other states to also visit Washington.

Shirlie sent along a statement addressed to concerned friends, mothers, and grandmothers. It told of plans to go to Washington, D.C., July 16 and 17. There, they would meet with legislators to express their complete and unalterable opposition to the Indochina War and to press for immediate action by elected officials to end it. They urged mothers across the nation to organize.

On July 10 she wrote to say that the mothers' delegation, which now numbered thirty, would be leaving the following week for Washington. They planned to hold meetings with various officials and a peaceful vigil in front of the White House.

The success of the WBZ talk show pointed out to me how important it was to reach out across the country. I resolved from then on to accept every chance to go public. Shortly before Michael died, I had written to a group called Another Mother for Peace, based in

Beverly Hills, California. I received a reply two days after learning of my son's death and joined the organization immediately.

In March 1971 Gene and I were contacted by Dorothy Jones, cochair of the group. She asked if we would take part in the production of a half-hour film to be shown on public television and around the country by peace groups. We agreed, and the filmmakers, headed by Donald MacDonald, came to our home.

The crew stayed with us for four days and nights. It was an enjoyable time. Most days were spent filming; we ate dinner late, then spent hours around the table drinking Gene's homemade wine and exchanging stories. It was good to laugh again after a year with so little humor in our lives. The two young men were bearded and long-haired, the lone young woman was a free spirit. The war protests had been born in California—they told of marching, singing, being arrested in front of federal buildings, and burning draft cards. Being a novice, I devoured every word.

On June 16 the film premiered in the Senate Theater in Washington, D.C. We had been sent plane tickets, so we left from Cedar Rapids on the 15th and checked into the Congressional Hotel. The next morning we were greeted by actress and fellow Iowan Donna Reed, a cochair of Another Mother for Peace. After breakfast and lunch with our charming hostess, we attended the afternoon screening.

I noticed in looking over the assembly that virtually none of the senators and representatives, all of whom had received special invitations, were present. They had control over the lives of our country's young men yet didn't want to look at what their protracted war was doing to the American family. Two senators did attend, Senator Hughes of Iowa, the only senator on the Armed Services Committee to dissent, and Senator Gruening of Alaska, one of two senators who had voted against President Johnson's Gulf of Tonkin resolution.

The thirty-minute film touched on the lives of five families who had been affected by the war in different ways. We represented a family whose son had been killed in Vietnam. In the film, we sit at the kitchen table and talk. Gene describes looking down from the roof of the house where he was repairing the antenna and seeing a marine sergeant and our parish priest getting out of a military car. He tells of asking three times: "Is my son dead?" Three times no one answered. There are scenes at the grave site—all silent. Back at the table Gene wonders how some men, with the passage of time, put the war aside when they leave it, while others carry it on to relive it with a kind of enjoyment when their sons grow to maturity and have to fight their generation's war.

Next, in East Covina, California, John Willy has been killed and his younger brother has decided not to face induction, breaking his family's tradition of military service.

The film then goes to Acton, Massachusetts, where a young man named Mark refuses to answer his draft call and enters a federal prison. He is the son of Quakers, his parents prisoners of their own proud consciences, supporting him tearlessly until it is time to say good-bye.

In Clearwater, Florida, we find a schoolteacher whose son is a prisoner in Hanoi. She has been removed from a teaching unit involving Southeast Asia because she can no longer be impartial.

The fifth family involved lives in College Station, Texas. The young husband lost his leg while serving with the marines in a war he didn't support. He wonders how it is that he was told to do many things which the Church of Christ had said were wrong.

One last statement from the teacher in Florida: "How can this be a government of the people when I don't know anyone in the country who is in favor of what our government is doing?"

When the film ended we were approached by Bess Myerson, also a member of the peace group. She gave me a message from a young veteran in the back of the theater. Gene and I went to talk to him.

Paul was dressed in fatigues and a military beret. Leaning against the seat beside him was a pair of crutches. He was nearly overcome with emotion but finally managed to explain to us that our son had been his friend for several weeks in Vietnam. Paul had trained Michael in jungle warfare.

About a month before Michael was killed, Paul had hit a land mine. He was in the hospital in Japan when Charlie Company was hit by friendly fire. Because of the film, he'd realized for the first time that his friend was dead. He told us he could always be found at the office of the Vietnam Veterans Against the War (VVAW) in Cambridge, Massachusetts.

In 1973 we drove out to Cambridge and asked for him at the VVAW. He was not in, but we made arrangements to take him to dinner the next day. To satisfy my own mind that this young man had really known Michael, I asked him several questions over dinner.

I remarked that there were probably several Michael Mullens in Vietnam. He looked up, gestured toward a black-and-white framed abstract photo on the wall, and said: "See that picture? His hair was that color." Michael's hair had begun to gray at seventeen or eighteen.

We never heard from Paul again, but he gave us one of his etchings of Vietnam scenes. It depicts a combat veteran dropping his rifle, with the caption, "Please, no more." When I look at the etching I think of Paul. He'd described his experiences in and out of veterans hospitals in the Northeast. As doctors prepared to amputate his leg, he'd climbed out of bed, called a taxi, and left. Because he'd refused the surgery, he could not receive government medical benefits. He was prepared to die—and I'm sure he did.

Over a year later, a letter arrived from Minnie Lee Gartley, mother of the POW in the film. Her son, Mark, was in the first group of prisoners to be released by Hanoi. We had recognized his name as he stepped from the plane bringing the first POWs back to their families, so we wrote to her. We wanted her to know we hadn't forgotten her and how happy we were for Mark and his family when we saw him step out of the plane.

The film had an impact throughout the state of Iowa, especially among private colleges and small-town peace groups. I was often invited to show the film, following it up with my plea to work for peace. After one screening, we received a letter from a woman in Cedar Falls, Iowa, who told us that people in her community had been deeply moved. She was convinced that those who saw the film would take steps to bring an end to this senseless war.

The Boston women from the WBZ radio show and I stayed in touch. In July 1971 I wrote to Shirlie and told her we were planning a vacation in the East and would stop to meet her family. When we knocked on their door two weeks later, we were welcomed with open arms. We sat at the kitchen table drinking gallons of coffee while an endless stream of neighbors flowed in and out the back door. The hospitality we felt in their kitchen was no different from that found in the farmhouse kitchens back in Iowa. We didn't go to a motel, and we wound up staying a week.

When I'd participated in the call-in program on WBZ from our home in Iowa, Jerry Williams had invited me to go live on his show if I ever came to Boston. My hosts notified him that I was in town, and a panel discussion was scheduled. We recruited two mothers who had lost sons in the war to sit on the panel with Gene and me. The women were nervous—they'd never been on a talk show. I assured them that one hostile response from a caller would cure their uneasiness. This was also Gene's first time, but he showed no concern. Our WBZ host was a seasoned professional and got the show off to a brisk start. The calls poured in for four hours.

The military and its supporters were relentless. They repeatedly accused us of dishonoring our fallen sons and acting like crybabies. After all, they argued, thousands of other mothers had lost sons, and they weren't going on talk shows to criticize our government and its policies.

At one point I found myself unable to answer a particularly angry caller. Gene smiled and handed me an envelope. On it, he had scribbled the words of an epitaph on a monument at Lexington dedicated to British soldiers who'd died there in the Revolutionary War. We'd visited there earlier in the day.

> They came 3000 miles and died
> To keep the past upon its throne
> Unheard, beyond the ocean tide
> Their English mother made her moan.
>
> April 19, 1775

This heart-rending verse worked magic, and the calls lost much of their heat.

When we returned home, we found another letter from Shirlie.

Dear Peg and Gene:

I can't begin to tell you how empty 93 Wendell Park seemed after you drove off—don't think I'm just saying that to be nice—David and I talked for a long time afterward about you and how great it was to meet comparative strangers, exchange ideas, live together, even though for a very short time, and feel as though we had been friends for years. So before you write to thank us, we want to thank you both so much for staying with us during your brief stay in Boston.

Please be sure and let us know when the article is going to appear in the *New Yorker* because I will want to buy several copies.

I am going to call Jerry Williams this afternoon and see if they will send you a tape of the broadcast.

So, my dears, once again thank you for your visit.

Shalom and love,
Shirlie

The WBZ broadcast resulted in more letters. Some pleaded for help in situations that required miracles. These were difficult for us. Any advice had to be given carefully, but I always urged these people to be relentless in their dealings with legislators—not to give up until they had gotten satisfaction. Military officials, I told them, were careful how they dealt with those in Congress who controlled their annual allotments. I always reminded them that their son belonged to *them*, not to the military.

One letter came from an inmate at a southern Michigan prison who wrote poetry. He was an ex-soldier who had served a five-year sentence for refusing to fight in Korea and who'd subsequently embarked on a life of crime. He admonished me to continue in what I was doing and not to give up as he had. He went on to say that our son must have been very proud of his parents and that he only wished that he had had such a father and mother. He expressed his sorrow over the loss of our son but added that we had gained many sons who loved us very much.

In the years following Michael's death I had asked myself many times whether I should continue trying to convince people that the war was wrong. This letter answered whatever doubt I had.

Also in the radio audience that night was a young veteran living in Massachusetts who wrote to tell me that thousands of listeners like himself were greatly moved by what all of us had to say. He, too, pleaded with us to keep on with our war protest and to never give up, adding that all Americans were enlightened because of what we were doing.

# EIGHT : PRIVATE ED HALL

Early one summer day our doorbell rang. I looked out the front window and saw an unfamiliar car in the driveway. I opened the door to a tall, handsome young man who asked if he could come in. When I hesitated, he blurted out, "But John McCormally said you'd talk to me." John was someone I'd met in the antiwar movement. He was the editor of the *Burlington Hawkeye* and a man I admired and respected. I extended my hand to the young man, invited him in, and asked if he'd share a cup of coffee with me.

It was still morning, so I prepared him breakfast. As soon as he'd eaten we took our cups of coffee to the living room—a beautiful room with large picture windows on the east and south walls and an unobstructed view for miles in either direction. Tom (not his real name) sat on an old-fashioned sewing rocker—an heirloom. He stared out the south window and rocked incessantly. I waited, and finally he began to talk.

He was a Vietnam veteran and a graduate of Grinnell College. When he returned from the war zone, he said, he felt he had a goal—a purpose. As he put it, "There must be peace." His plan was to contact other peace-seeking people all over the United States. He wanted to charter an airliner and fly to the capitals of the world's nations to meet with their leaders. He had no doubt he would succeed. Unfortunately, he restated his plans over and over for about three hours—almost as if he had been programmed. I couldn't decide whether he was mentally ill or simply high on drugs.

Gene had slept late that morning, after working four hours' overtime the day before. When he awoke, I invited Tom to join us in the kitchen for lunch. The two visited until it was time for Gene to leave for work. I then told Tom that he would have to go. (I was afraid to be alone with him.) He thanked me and promised to keep in touch.

Thoughts of the young visitor lingered the rest of the day. When the phone rang that evening, I wasn't surprised that the call was about Tom. The caller was Dr. Joseph Wall, dean at Grinnell College. He wanted to know if Tom had been to our house. Apparently, he'd sneaked away from home while on leave from the Veterans Hospital. When his mother discovered her son was missing, she drove to Grinnell in search of him. I promised Dr. Wall that I'd contact him immediately if I heard from Tom again.

At about 8 P.M. the phone rang again—it was Tom. "Please, Mrs. Mullen," he said, "I need you and Gene. Please come and pick me up at the Holiday Inn in Cedar Rapids." I explained I would have to drive fifteen miles to Waterloo to pick up Gene and then another seventy-five miles to Cedar Rapids. "Will you promise to stay there?" I asked. He promised, and I believed him.

I phoned Grinnell College and relayed the information to the dean. Tom's mother, accompanied by some friends, drove to Cedar Rapids and picked up her son. Dr. Wall phoned later to say that the young man was on his way home but would probably be spending the rest of his life in an institution. Tom, he told me, had been a brilliant student who graduated with honors.

One evening recently I decided to see if I could learn how the past twenty years had treated Tom. I found Dr. Wall in retirement at the college. He was pleased to tell me that Tom had regained his health, is very happy, and works as a legal aide in a large law firm. I wonder if he remembers his "dream" plan.

After spending the few hours with Tom and learning firsthand how the war was destroying great minds, I became more determined than ever to come to the aid of returned veterans. We first learned of Private Ed Hall when men of Michael's unit began to write and drop by for visits when they returned stateside. At that time, the private was serving a two-and-a-half-year sentence as a result of his behavior following the incident that killed Michael.

We got involved in Ed's case with the conviction that we would right another wrong. We wrote to him at Fort Leavenworth, Kansas, then made arrangements to see him while on a trip to Kansas City to visit our children, Mary and John, at Rockhurst College.

We called ahead to confirm our visit for ten o'clock Saturday morning. Arriving early, we spent thirty minutes driving around the fort. The grounds were beautiful, even though the War College for the Army was located next to the federal prison. The homes of the officers were built of red brick, and the streets were lined with massive oak trees. The fort was established as an early western military outpost in 1827 and named after its first commander, Colonel Henry Leavenworth.

As we entered the reception hall, an officer told us that the young soldier we came to see had been put in solitary confinement the day before and would not be allowed visitors. Gene and I had gone many miles out of our way. The men in charge had plenty of time to notify us of this change. We told the officer that we intended to see Hall, then we dropped the name of our favorite senator, Harold Hughes, who was serving on the Armed Services Committee. The officer relented.

Before meeting Private Hall we asked to see a psychiatrist familiar with his case. John and Mary had come along, John with a beard and long hair, Mary with plate-sized sunglasses. The doctor kept referring to "today's young people" and how difficult they were to handle and understand, while casting suspicious glances at our offspring. I assured him that we liked young people—found them intelligent, informed, and well behaved. We tried to convince him that Ed Hall needed counseling, not imprisonment, and asked why no one was helping him. Unfortunately, the time we spent with the psychiatrist was a total waste.

We didn't have any trouble understanding Hall or his attitude. He'd grown up in a tough neighborhood in Detroit and had managed to complete three years of high school before getting a job with General Motors. He deeply resented being drafted and sent to Vietnam. Many blacks faced the same problems in uniform as they had in the outside world.

Hall had made no effort to adjust to the mud, the leeches, the slime, or to humping everything everywhere, instead of going by helicopters as he saw other units go. He was small, and his pack was always too heavy.

During our many visits to Ed Hall we spent most of the time talking about the incident that killed Michael and put Hall in jail. The February 17 mission began early in the morning, and much of the time the soldiers waded through waist-deep rice paddies infested with leeches. They were forced to hump extra ammo for the artillery. Hall seemed to slip and fall more than the other men, and with his extra load he had to be helped up.

Private Hall fell once too often and had endured all the derision he could. He lost control, threw his pack down, and refused his officer's command to move. He told us how Michael, his only white friend in Charlie Company, stepped between him and the angry officer, put Hall's extra pack on his own back, and continued to shield the errant private until they dug in for the night.

When Hall awoke to the carnage of falling shrapnel, he found his lone friend dying and the man on his other side screaming in agony. He leaned against a tree and retched. Upon learning a few minutes later that their own artillery had shelled them, he had to be restrained from harming the forward observer.

He told us how he brooded for days; the only soldier who could have helped him was dead. He didn't know he went berserk until he woke up several days later, in a hospital bed and under arrest. They told him that he had fired on Vietnamese rice farmers, thrown hand grenades, pulled a gun on the sergeant who had replaced Michael, and struck an officer. He learned that it had taken several men to subdue him, and in doing so he had been oversedated, causing his heart to stop.

Hall had a copy of his court-martial, which he gave to me on one of our visits. I took it home and pored over it for days. I read that the pretrial investigation had taken only one day and that the trial itself lasted less than four hours. The incident that killed two and wounded ten men was not mentioned during the trial. We had already asked for an investigation of Michael's death before Hall came to trial and felt that this influenced the outcome. Gene and I enlisted the help of Michigan Senator Philip Hart, and Hall was given a new military attorney to investigate why the first lawyer had not probed into the cause of Hall's erratic behavior.

Hall was eventually discharged. Two or three years later he called us from New Orleans. He said he was in trouble with his wife—she'd left him—and he wanted to come to Iowa and stay with us. He was still living with problems that followed him from Vietnam, so we told him not to come. We had spent hours trying to counsel disturbed veterans who made their way to our home. Some responded, but many didn't seem to benefit from these visits. We knew we could not deal with Ed Hall.

Private Hall had been a great storyteller. During our visits to the prison we spent our time in the courtyard, a comfortable recreation ground furnished with picnic tables and benches. Visitors gathered there from all parts of the country. Whites always seemed to be in the minority, greatly outnumbered by blacks. One Sunday afternoon, a large party of blacks enjoyed a picnic. Peals of laughter filled the air, and the mood was very upbeat. Ed told us happily that the older man in the group had come to Leavenworth in his private jet to take his son home. The father was a prominent criminal attorney in St. Louis. His son had been court-martialed in Vietnam for raping the madam of a whorehouse in Saigon. The sentence was three years of hard labor, but it had taken the father only a few weeks to free his son.

While we ate our lunch, Hall pointed to a cell window off in the distance. "See that soldier in the barred window," he said. "He has quite a past."

As an Air Force major, the prisoner had been command pilot for Ellsworth Bunker, U.S. ambassador to Vietnam. He'd been apprehended at Tan Son Nhut Air Base outside Saigon with $8 million worth of heroin in his aircraft and $25,000 in cash. At that time, Hall told us, Bunker's wife was the American ambassador to Thailand. Because the pilot flew there weekends, it was very convenient for his crew to carry on lucrative drug operations.

The men at Leavenworth particularly enjoyed the story of the major, as it reinforced their belief that the entire structure of the war had been corrupted. (I later learned that Bunker's wife, Carol C. Laise, was actually U.S. ambassador to Nepal.) Every veteran had his own special story of corruption. Many told of being introduced to marijuana for the first time by their officers. Others told how their lockers were looted at base camp while the grunts were in the field. The black market flourished.

As we left the prison one afternoon, we noticed a young woman waiting for a city bus. She was sobbing quietly. I approached her and asked if we could be of help. She said she was waiting for the bus into town, so we offered her a ride to her motel. Between sobs Maria told us her story.

Her husband, Richard, had been in the service for four years, most of it spent in Germany where he worked as a chaplain's assistant. Maria had lived with him there. The young couple was preparing to return to the States for discharge. One evening Richard found it necessary to go to his office on business. On his way he passed through the barracks and encountered a group of soldiers. Suddenly, MPs rushed in and arrested the startled young man while the entire group of soldiers escaped out the windows.

Richard was accused of dealing drugs and after a short court-martial proceeding was sentenced to three years of hard labor. The chaplain had tried to help his former assistant but had been thwarted at every turn. He was transferred to the States before he could testify in Richard's behalf.

Maria insisted her husband was innocent. She had ridden a bus from New York City and was exhausted. We suggested she ride home with us, rest for a few days, and continue on her trip to New York. She wanted to accept our invitation but said she had to return to the prison Sunday and would let us know at that time. The next day we took her back to the prison to meet her husband. They sat at a table across the courtyard; he looked over at us and nodded his assent.

We left Sunday evening for the five-hour ride home. During the trip she told us about her life as a Puerto Rican growing up in a New York City ghetto. She and Richard fell in love as teenagers and married young. They were both ambitious. Before he went into the army he was the owner of a successful house-painting business. Neither of them had ever been in trouble. They'd been devastated by the accusations leading to the court-martial. She said the only conclusion her husband could draw was that he may have unwittingly uncovered a drug ring led by his commanding officer.

When we got to the farm I suggested to Maria that she take a hot bath while I fixed her something to eat. I later put her to bed with a cup of hot chocolate. She rested all day Monday. On Tuesday we took her to Waterloo and put her on the bus for New York and the Bronx. Saying good-bye was like sending one of our own daughters off to school.

Victims of military justice entered our lives regularly—many for only a few brief moments, and then they were lost forever. On May 18 I wrote her a short letter:

> Dear Maria:
>
> We watched the clock this morning and heaved a sigh of relief when it was 11 A.M., your time 12 noon, and realized you were back in the city.
>
> Today I talked to an aide in Senator Hart's office, and they assured me they would be able to help Ed Hall. I told them we would hire an attorney, if necessary—his aide urged us not to and reassured me they would take care of everything.
>
> After talking to Hart's office and finding them receptive to my request to help Ed Hall, I began to think about your Richard. I'd suggest you write to Senator Jacob Javits, even if he could get a few weeks off the three-year sentence, it would enable you to start working for an Honorable Discharge.
>
> Today, I dropped a postcard to your Richard, telling him that we had put you on the bus to return home.
>
> It was nice meeting you, and maybe the next time we meet your life and world will be back to normal.
>
> Peg Mullen

On May 21 we received a final word from Maria:

> Dear Mrs. Mullen:
>
> I must apologize for my delay. Please don't think I'm ungrateful or forgetful. It's just that I've been so very busy from the minute I arrived in N.Y. As you remember I am staying with Richard's

sister. Anyway, I called home as soon as I arrived and learned that her baby had been born an hour after I left for Kansas City.

The trip wasn't too bad and I found a nice lady who made the trip with me. It's hard because I'm constantly thinking of Richard and I miss him more than ever. I've really never been able to believe or accept what has happened. It's just a bad nightmare and I haven't awakened. I live in a fantasy world. I try to face up to my problems as best as I can.

I see that you've gone to work for Mr. Hall. I'm glad and I'm sure he will always be grateful to you and Mr. Mullen. It's really a wonder that there are people like you.

As for my dilemma I will just sit and wait. If by August they haven't done anything for Richard then I will get in touch with you, and we'll see what can be done. I don't want to stir things up unless I have no choice. I've waited this long so might as well hold on a little while longer. I'm sure you will agree.

Once again thank you for your help and understanding. It was a wonderful experience meeting you and I hope we can meet again.

Sincerely,<br>
Maria

# NINE : I GO TO SEE THE PRESIDENT

In late February 1971, when an announcement came from the White House that President Nixon would attend a farm conference in Des Moines and address the legislature, Iowa—a Republican state in the Bible Belt—was already in a state of anger. Most Iowans, indeed most midwesterners, had had their fill of six years of broken promises from their president. Farmers were unhappy with the farm policy, and labor was tired of its bashing at the hands of the administration. Mothers enraged over continuation of the war in Vietnam were backed by thousands of students making their voices heard on campuses across the state.

Plans were laid by all the groups to amass in Des Moines to protest against the president, a man who campaigned, and won, in

1968 on a platform to bring an end to the Vietnam War. Organized labor had their agenda, as did the Farmer's Union from South Dakota, North Dakota, Nebraska, and Minnesota, whose members came in chartered buses. The Farmer's Union was joined by busloads of the National Farmer's Organization from the lower midwestern states. The Mothers for Peace and students across the state of Iowa carefully planned their strategy.

On the eve of the president's visit, I received a call from a young state senator who told me that he was planning to interrupt Nixon's speech at the capitol and attempt to present him with a signed petition for an immediate end to the Vietnam War. I asked him why he had called me and particularly why he had exposed his plan over the telephone. He responded that I was the only one he had called. I quickly told him of our suspicions that our phone was tapped. Within an hour after his call, the FBI moved in on the senator and warned him that if he made the slightest move during the president's speech he would be forcefully removed from the capitol chambers. This certainly bolstered the claim that our telephone had been tapped. Nixon's paranoia had reared its ugly head in the heartland of the USA.

For my part in the protest, I prepared a sign that read: "55,000 dead, 300,000 wounded, my son, just one." A close friend, Sister Mary Richard, a Notre Dame nun who taught at our local parochial school, came for dinner the night before our trip to Des Moines. We spent the evening working on my poster. I gave her the words; she did the art work. The poster was large, 4 x 6 feet, and would be ungainly to carry. We reinforced the back by gluing on several handles from six-pack beer cartons. The extra handles would give me more security.

While we worked, the two of us speculated about whether there would be a crowd—and remembered that only one year ago Michael's stilled body had come home. There were no Secret Service agents to guard the precious cargo, and there were no masses of people to greet his return.

Early on Monday six of us, three mothers and three students, left for Des Moines by car. When we reached the statehouse lawn, I was elated and amazed at the number of people that emptied out of the buses and cars to join the swelling crowd on the capitol grounds. To me, the crowd appeared to be mostly middle-aged. There were farmers and union members with their spouses. And there were mothers of all ages, some close to seventy-five years of age. At last we had a

**Just One . . .**

The mother of an American killed in the Indochina war adds her protest to those of several thousand workers, farmers and other citizens against the war during Monday's Des Moines visit by President Nixon.

*This photograph accompanied a front-page story on President Nixon's visit to Des Moines in the University of Iowa student newspaper on March 2, 1971. Photo by Diane Hypes, reprinted with permission of the* Daily Iowan, *© 1994.*

group of concerned fathers and mothers who were joining their sons and daughters in protest. With a crowd estimated at several thousand, it was probably the largest protest of this kind ever held in the state.

Of course, I realized that many in the crowd were not there primarily to protest the war, but their presence did give me a feeling of security. I felt it would be difficult for Nixon, the press, and the Secret Service to ignore this gray-haired mass of Middle Americans. Almost everyone carried a sign. We had read for years about the obscene posters carried in the antiwar marches, but the messages appearing on the statehouse lawn that day went beyond anything a peace group had ever produced.

Those carried by the labor group were strongly worded and insulting, indicating a new resentment of attacks on them by the Republican administration. The farmers' signs told of their years of hardship from low market prices. And then there were the signs held high over their heads by the Mothers for Peace: "War Is Not Healthy for Children and Other Living Things."

I remember standing on the steps at the west entrance of the capitol, looking down Walnut Avenue as far as I could see, wondering where the people were . . . the people that should have been on the streets to greet and welcome the president. There was only a scattering. I'm sure many of the president's supporters stayed home because of the planned protest.

The ride for the president from the airport to the capitol followed Grand Avenue from west to east through the Des Moines business district. Then came a gradual uphill climb of several blocks to the capitol itself, with its golden dome glistening in the morning sun. As the motorcade approached its destination, it must have been apparent to Nixon and his party that the streets were not crowded. As the presidential limousine neared the capitol, a mob of thousands began to make its protest against the war, singing and shouting obscenities, surging toward the president's car. It was necessary for the driver to make a sudden change in direction. He sped up and drove quickly toward the rear of the building and into the underground parking.

Suddenly the protestors realized that the president was going to bypass them. The crowd poured around the building to the east entrance, but he had already entered the building and was safe on the podium. The president, with his usual aplomb, raised his voice above the din of the shouting mob and delivered his message to the state legislature and friends.

Most of us remember the Vietnam cry: "One, two, three, four! We don't want your fucking war." As many times as I'd marched, I could not bring myself to utter the favorite four-letter word to describe the war. I wondered whether there might be another, more acceptable, term that could be applied. But when a very elderly woman next to me turned and asked, "Isn't this just terrible?" I heard myself shout, above the noise of the crowd, "You're fucking right." I attribute that outburst to mob psychology. I never became comfortable with the word and did not use it again.

As Nixon emerged from the east side of the capitol, I feared that he would go into his arm-waving "Eisenhower greeting" and that he might even flash the peace sign, as he'd done recently in California. When he raised his arm in salute, a wave of protest rolled across the grounds, filling the air for blocks around. I kept asking myself: "Is this actually happening? Is this the president of the United States who is being booed?"

Nixon brought down his right arm and dropped to his haunches as he carefully made his way down the steps, completely covered by his Secret Service men until he was safely in the car. The scene will remain with me forever. As the car hurried away from the crowd, it was pelted with snowballs. The president later described the incident to the press as "all in good fun."

My group took its time leaving the capitol grounds, and we walked slowly to our car several blocks away. Instead of driving back to Waterloo, we decided to go downtown to the Hotel Fort Des Moines, where the farm conference was in session. When we arrived we found the entire block facing the hotel entrance lined with people of all ages. It appeared that each person had his or her own private message held high on a placard.

I remember seeing an ambulance and its crew standing in readiness close to the hotel, and I wondered, "What have we become in this country—when an ambulance has to stand in waiting while the president makes an appearance?"

Fearing a repeat of the scene at the capitol, the local police had lined up city buses, nose-to-rear, for one block on either side of the street, so that Nixon's limousine was able to drive through the corridor in safety. The crowd swelled across Tenth Street and into the next block. The chants echoed and re-echoed and, I'm sure, must have penetrated the walls of the conference room inside the hotel.

The young people were not alone—everywhere I turned were fathers and mothers. The men wore short haircuts. The women were gray-haired, and several wore black veils of mourning. I visited with two sturdy grandmothers.

We were unlikely participants in such a demonstration. I suppose we should have been flattered that the press later reported us as twenty-year-olds. As I stood visiting with a friend, a professor's wife who had come with me from Cedar Falls, we suddenly found ourselves pushed to the corner of the Tenth Street intersection. We noticed a flurry of activity among the television crews, and instantly the air was filled with white objects. Then it happened. A flying wedge of police began to move into the edge of the crowd, and I remember thinking, "Is this how it was at Kent State?"

In an instant I made plans to protect myself, and as I looked up I faced a line of police coming toward me with a length of 2 x 4 lumber as a wedge, shouting orders to move back. Standing with a street barricade at my back, I wasn't sure that I wanted to move. I put my sign up both for protection and in defiance and found myself fighting for a square of cardboard that somehow had become very precious to me.

Without warning, I was in hand-to-hand combat with a plainclothes officer. When he realized that no power on earth could take the sign from me, he raised his right arm high and came down across my face with his elbow. He began clubbing me with his nightstick, and only the street barricade behind me kept me from falling to the pavement. At one point during the confrontation I noticed a live microphone held close to my face. I looked up, muttering, "Oh, no." A young reporter asked, "Are you Peg?" and when I nodded, he withdrew, telling me not to worry. Soon two young student marshals came to help me make a retreat. I remember shouting at the gentleman who grappled with me that next time there would be a thousand mothers with me, not just one! My sign came home intact.

During the struggle I hadn't been overly concerned with the man's flying fists and elbows, but the madness in his eyes seared into my mind. Committed to the protection of the president, I'm sure he could have killed in the line of duty. But if the officer had lost control, I knew that I, too, had allowed myself to reach his level. The hate that he saw in my face and eyes was probably equal to his.

As I retreated from the melee, I watched a cameraman being clubbed by two men, while another smashed every piece of his equipment. His father was an activist in the antiwar movement and a friend of mine. I turned to look for my friend from Cedar Falls and, to my horror, saw her being dragged by her long hair down the street on her back. Then four men rushed out of the Firestone agency, struggled with her attackers, picked up the bedraggled woman, and took her into their building. She suffered no injuries, but her dignity was badly bruised.

It was almost an hour before the ropes and barricades were removed so we could go to our cars. A middle-aged woman was circulating among the angry students and mothers, passing out literature and telling us that we must return to God—only he could right the wrongs. Her literature warned about the evils of Communism. I suggested to her that perhaps we should fight Communism at home, rather than in Indochina, and that maybe we should start in the Pentagon. She regarded me with a puzzled look. "What and where is the Pentagon?"

As we walked to the parking lot, I found myself face-to-face with Dan Rather, then assigned to the White House beat, who was waiting outside the Hotel Fort Des Moines for the president to emerge. I looked at him in disgust and asked, "How can you travel with this man?"

"Lady, do you think I enjoy it?" he responded.

The national media in general gave little coverage to the massive protest. During the episode on the capitol grounds the correspondents had somehow been locked in their press bus. As I watched them beating on the windows with fists, even shoes, in an attempt to escape, I desperately wished for a camera to record this humorous scene in a world of madness that surrounded the president's appearance in Des Moines, Iowa, March 1, 1971.

On our drive home, an older woman in our group kept repeating that the confrontation had recalled the nightmare she had lived through thirty years before in Germany, with the club-swinging Iowa police taking on the image of Hitler's dreaded SS. She later told me that she had spent the entire next day crying hysterically. The young people with us shrugged it off as "typical Nixon." Indeed, the president himself remarked to the press that evening that it had all been "about par for the course."

# TEN : THE DRAFT

"I'm writing as one mother to another, but with a great difference—your son accepted his 'duty' and died for it. My son is refusing to accept it." The writer quoted her youngest son: "Mom, I have given this considerable thought—believe me—and I can only come to one conclusion. I will have nothing, I repeat, nothing to do with our military system as it stands now. I love my country . . . I would fight to death to defend it if we were invaded, but how can I pick up a gun and shoot someone who means me no harm?" She ended her letter, "What do I say to a draft dodger? What can I—as a mother—do?"

Every letter I received was answered in my own handwriting. Though I didn't keep copies of my replies, I've no doubt how I answered this troubled mother. I'm certain I told her my regret for not having shown Michael how to evade the draft. I hope that when she looks back on the war she still supports her son's decision to defend himself from being sacrificed. Because he made that choice, he is alive today.

John Mahon writes in his book *History of the Militia and the National Guard*: "Early in the United States involvement in Vietnam, President Johnson decided not to mobilize the reserves and to rely on draftees to fight in Asia. In making this decision he overruled both Secretary McNamara and the Joint Chiefs of Staff who wanted to order at least 200,000 reservists into federal service."

One of the major reasons for Johnson's decision was to conceal from the American people the high level of military commitment the nation was making in a distant land. Mahon states: "Because the National Guard was scarcely used in Vietnam, it became a refuge for men who sought to escape being drafted into that war. The war in Vietnam was over for Guardsmen by mid-June 1969, four years before the last American troops left the area."

During the long years of the Vietnam War the draft loomed ominously for every American male as he approached his eighteenth birthday. It was always there, standing squarely between him and his future plans. In Michael's case, those plans had involved agricultural research. At age eighteen, he believed the country soon would no longer be able to feed its standard grains to livestock—that by the year 2000 it would become necessary to use them all to feed the world's starving masses.

Draft boards in each county were appointed, and in many cases, these appointments were political. The board members, usually men, often found it difficult to be totally unbiased—many were tempted with bribes or pleas from close friends whose sons were subject to the draft. In 1970 the chairman of our county draft board, a professor at the University of Northern Iowa, had four draft-age sons. All of them were occupationally deferred to teach school, even though there was no shortage of teachers. One of his sons taught in our local school and was heard to boast that he didn't worry about the draft.

On May 5, 1970, the sister-in-law of an Iowan soldier wrote me: "My husband's brother is now in Cambodia with the 1st Air Cavalry. He was drafted by Buchanan County . . . after several months of protest because of his father's heart condition. He was doing all the farm work and was the sole support of his family." The young man had been drafted April 1, 1969, and his father died the following day. Still, he received no deferment. The draftee was wounded in November and returned to action on Christmas Day. One month later a news item appeared in the *Waterloo Courier*:

> Fairbank—A rural Fairbank soldier serving in Cambodia has been killed in action, according to word received by his family.
>
> Mrs. Mary Clayton said Thursday she had received word that her son had been fatally wounded when his army unit encountered enemy opposition in the Cambodian campaign.
>
> His father died April 2, 1969, the day after his son was drafted.
>
> Spec. Clayton, . . . a grenade launch carrier, was a 1967 Jesup High School graduate and attended Hawkeye Technical Institute in Waterloo before he was drafted. He had been in Vietnam since last September and was recently sent into Cambodia.

The Buchanan County draft board was typical of rural midwestern draft boards, which were obsessed with filling monthly quotas. Elsewhere in the country, many states made no attempt to fill them. California, for example, never surpassed 60 percent. To make up for conscription shortfalls in those states, it was necessary to draft vigorously elsewhere, principally in the Farm Belt, the city ghettos, and Appalachia. The death count from the states of Iowa and West Virginia stood in grim testimony to this fact. The final death count for Iowa was 852 and for West Virginia, 731.

While waiting for Michael's body we drove to Buchanan County to visit a mother who had just lost a son. She was on welfare and living in stark poverty. There was no evidence of food being brought in by friends and relatives; in contrast, our community fed us for ten days. She had been abandoned in her sorrow. The boy she was to bury the next day was the third of her sons to be sent to Vietnam. As tears streamed down her face, she told of praying her first two boys home safely. But when her third son was drafted, she said, she could pray no longer, and thus he was abandoned to die. Looking for a ray of light in her shattered life, she told us the draft board chairman had called to say they would not draft her remaining son. I was so enraged I had to leave this stricken mother.

As the war dragged on it became common for draft boards to bend rules and overlook a name here and there. More states fell short of quotas, as it became impossible to reach them. Draft counseling became available at most public universities and private campuses. Michael's undergraduate college, a private school which received support from war industries in Missouri, did not offer counseling.

By 1969, because of the uproar over the unfairness of the draft coming from college students who could not plan for their future and the poor who couldn't escape the draft, the U.S. government changed to a lottery system. The order of induction depended on the chance drawing of birth dates. Those with low numbers were subject to induction, allowing the lucky ones with high numbers to go on with their lives.

Often young men who had been receiving college deferments were drafted. Because the war dragged on for ten years, many of them, after four or five years of deferment, found themselves in the line of fire—as 1st lieutenants facing a four-year stint in the service. Many were made platoon leaders and died by the hundreds. Those who declined advanced training were sent immediately to the jungle with no consideration of their qualifications. Their chances for survival were slim.

In April 1970 a distressed young college student wrote that he was well aware of the draft because he had lost his student deferment. He was not alone. His roommate came from a farm, and "his number in the draft lottery means he'll be gone by June . . . to become cannon fodder." He added that many others would eventually submit, swallowed up by words like duty, honor, and country. He closed his remarkable letter by telling me that he was not "a radical, yippie, hippie, or any of those other stereotyped phrases. I just relish my rights and freedoms—God-given—not Nixon-given."

Promotions for the draftee bearing the brunt of the warfare were almost nonexistent—advancements were given to enlisted army personnel, many safe at their desks at the rear. These men needed to be rewarded so they would continue to serve. Draftees were anxious to put their service behind them and couldn't be counted on to re-enlist. On January 16, 1970, Michael wrote me that he was being made platoon sergeant. He was growing bitter. "The bullshit is getting worse," he said, "almost as bad as stateside."

When he died, I determined from the amount of his final pay voucher that he had not, in fact, been promoted but had served in the capacity of acting platoon sergeant for a few weeks, pending the arrival of a sergeant with more service time. We were somewhat amused when, after we'd complained about the inadequate compensation he'd received for his last eighteen days, he was posthumously promoted to platoon sergeant.

There were many ways to obtain deferments. The country was full of doctors who considered the war immoral and were willing to falsify medical records. In Michael's case, he was beset with allergies he'd acquired from working with white rats in research. The week before his induction physical, he visited the physician who had taken care of him since he was two years old.

The doctor, who had worked at an induction center during World War II, told him he'd have no problems. With his noticeable allergies, no one would give him a clean bill of health. But the red-rimmed watery eyes and drippy nose went unnoticed by the examining doctor at the induction center, and Michael had no written statement from his personal physician.

One young man from New Jersey who had drawn a low number in the lottery had better luck when he went for his physical. According to his sister, a local doctor had placed the young man on a grapefruit and vitamin diet, and his weight dropped from 140 to 115 pounds. On hearing that he had failed his physical, she wrote, the family had the biggest, loudest, and most tearful celebration they ever had.

Some young men were able to obtain conscientious objector status. Unfortunately, this status did not always keep them from the rigors of combat. Many of them served as medics in the field, performing heroic acts in rescuing wounded men under fire, tending the dying, and sometimes giving their own lives. "I don't know why I'm writing" a young man from West Virginia began his letter:

> I was raised in a small town in the industrial Ohio Valley . . . and believed that we should be in Vietnam to fight for democracy. Then, Kent State. Then it hit me.
>
> I was told by the local draft board that I didn't have the background to apply as a conscientious objector, although I knew that I could not kill.
>
> Following graduation, I was drafted. I made a last-minute, though sincere, plea for conscientious objector status. My willingness to perform alternate service persuaded my draft board to approve [it]. It was not an easy decision, nor was the alternate service

an easy task. One co-worker even told me that my desk job wasn't punishment enough for what I had done.

A mother who had raised her six children as Jehovah's Witnesses in the Smoky Mountains in Tennessee wrote me concerning her oldest son:

> He came before the draft board and gave a scriptural reason for not going to war. He was no weakling. It took courage to stand before a courtroom full of people and make a defense for his life. He did not run off to Canada.
>
> He was sentenced to two years in prison in Tallahassee, Florida. So if it is any consolation one of the Jehovah's Witnesses did not shoot your son, Michael.

Inequities in the Selective Service System caused bitterness among neighbors, friends, and even families. One woman from Cedar Rapids, Iowa, wrote us in April 1970 complaining of unfairness in the Selective Service process. She said her son, an infantryman, was still having nightmares about his Vietnam experience. Meanwhile, several other local families had sent their sons to college, where they got teaching certificates. "I guess it wouldn't seem so bad if everyone 'felt' the cost of the war," she added. "Only two houses away people may not know or care that you have a son in Vietnam. The 'war' does not touch them. Others who have sons of military age don't even seem concerned—we have many times felt so desperately alone."

Only a corrupt system would countenance such inequities. By the end of the war, public sentiment against the draft had grown so strong that the government was forced to seek alternatives. The result was an all-volunteer army under the leadership of General William Westmoreland. The feasibility of an all-volunteer army came under serious consideration as the country faced unknown odds in the Persian Gulf. There was concern over our ability to back up the regular forces and reserves in the event of great losses. However, the Defense Department and White House were adamant in their decision to risk it with volunteers.

Had there been a draft in operation during the Persian Gulf campaign, I believe there would have been a massive outcry against our involvement. There would have been a lot less flag-waving and patriotic posturing had another whole generation of Americans been suddenly placed at risk. As it happened, only a very small number of our young men and women were involved, and, in most instances, it had been their choice to go. Only a minute segment of our population was directly affected.

In March 1974 I made a plea for unconditional amnesty for draft evaders. The previous month, I had received a call from Iowa Congressman Edward Mezvinsky, inviting me to testify at hearings to be held March 6, 11, and 13 by a subcommittee of the House Judiciary Committee. The invitation didn't surprise me. I had publicly expressed my views regarding amnesty on several occasions. I was flattered, but I panicked at the thought of having to sit alone at a table in the hearing room and deliver a statement before such a formidable panel. Mezvinsky wouldn't take no, so I yielded and began making plans to go to Washington. I rejected his offer to travel by plane and decided on a bus trip. I had to have time to relax and prepare myself. This was to be the greatest challenge I'd confronted since Michael's death.

I needed a professional statement, so I went to C. D. B. Bryan, who was in the process of writing *Friendly Fire*, and asked for his help. He phoned me later with remarks which I took down in shorthand. Afterward, Bryan was upset because I had not given him credit for writing the piece. I reminded him that everyone in public office, particularly presidents, employed speechwriters, and I didn't think it was wrong not to tell the public that I had asked for his assistance. I spent several hours studying the statement, changing a word occasionally so it would sound like Peg Mullen. I felt it would have tremendous impact if I could deliver it.

The trip to D.C. took twenty-four hours. For part of the ride, I sat with a Boston family whose son had been ordained a Roman Catholic priest the previous week at the University of Notre Dame. The young priest agreed wholeheartedly with my stand for amnesty and treated me to breakfast at 3 A.M. in Cleveland. The entire family wished me luck.

I arrived in D.C. Sunday evening and went directly to the Capitol Hill Hotel, where I was going to room with Pat Simon from Boston. She, too, had lost a son in Vietnam. (We had met previously in the peace movement.) She had testified on Friday and wanted to share her experience with me. She said she'd been a basket case by the time she approached the panel and sat down in front of the cameras. She was an educated school principal but still was frightened.

Pat returned to Boston early Monday. Later that morning, I walked alone to the nearby Rayburn House Office Building and went directly to the hearing room. There I met Father John Smith, a professor from St. Ambrose College in Davenport, Iowa. Congressman Mezvinsky had decided I would be more comfortable if Father Smith sat with me while I testified. I picked up the agenda and found to my horror that Father and I would be the last to appear. We would have a long wait.

I don't know how I got through that day. At lunch with Mezvinsky and Father Smith, I could barely swallow. I'd always wanted to sample the Capitol's famous bean soup, but I had to push it aside. At 4:30 I was finally called to testify. I sat down next to Father, comforted somehow by his presence, and whispered to myself, "Michael, you got me into this, and you damn well better get me out of it." The lights were on, the cameras rolling. I looked up to the panel and began.

"Thank you. My son, Michael Mullen, was killed four years ago in Vietnam by our own artillery. He was killed, in military terminology, by friendly fire and was, therefore, a nonhostile casualty because of an artillery incident officially referred to as a misadventure in a war that was undeclared. He was twenty-five years old."

I paused, and from directly behind my chair I heard: "Listen to this one. It's going to be great. She's going to give them hell." I'd worried about the audience response in a hearing-room setting, but this small show of support was all I needed. My fear and panic melted away. I continued.

"Now, we are an ordinary family. We are just simple Iowa farmers, and we are not hampered or confused by the political considerations, nor the political motivations, nor political expediences that you are, so we can speak plainly. We know and can accept what you politicians are still simply unwilling to admit and that is that the war in Vietnam which took our son was a senseless, terrible, tragic blunder, and now we see that you want to compound this mistake by punishing further those young men who refused to be deluded by your war from the beginning.

"Gentlemen, the whole Vietnam War was a misadventure. We are all its nonbattle casualties. Only those who have lost sons and husbands and brothers in Vietnam can understand the depth of the anguish and the bitterness my son's death makes me feel. I want to believe—I desperately need to believe that my son's life was not wasted, that he died for some high ideal, but what comfort have you given me?"

At this point in the presentation, I scanned the audience to the left and saw a woman actually shedding tears. And I realized that my voice was the only sound in the room. I took a deep breath and continued.

"If Congress is going to insist on misinterpreting amnesty as meaning to pardon, then the amnesty issue will remain too emotionally charged ever to be resolved. A pardon implies guilt, and I would no more expect a young man who refused to kill in Vietnam, whose profound moral and spiritual opposition to that war left him no alternative but to leave the country, to admit that he was guilty of a crime, than I would expect Congress, than I would expect you, whose support of that war permitted it to endure for so long, at so dreadful a cost in young lives, to admit that it, too, was guilty of a crime.

"Amnesty, in its original Greek, meant forgetfulness. Forget that these young men left rather than served. Forget the draft inequities that forced them to leave. Forget the lies—and I repeat—the lies told you by the presidents, the generals, the spokesmen for the State Department and the Pentagon. Forget all the moral and philosophical dilemmas posed by the war in Vietnam which tore this nation apart for over a dozen years. Remember only this: the American people have suffered enough because of this war, and we want our children home.

"Vietnam's dilemmas cannot be resolved, but only a fool still believes 'My country right or wrong.' We all now understand that if our country is wrong, we, as citizens, have an obligation to correct it. Who is the more loyal citizen: the one who agonizes over his nation's policies and attempts to change them, or is docile acceptance of governmental policy—no matter how immoral and misguided—the most acceptable, the truer mark of a loyal citizen?

"If it is the former, then you cannot and must not punish those young American citizens whose unwillingness to take part in the war in Vietnam was based on a high sense of allegiance and responsibility to America's ideals. If it is the latter, if the mark of good citizenship is docile submission to government policy, then all those convicted and imprisoned and executed at Nuremberg for war crimes should have been freed.

"In 1964 the American people voted for that presidential candidate whom they believed would most swiftly bring that war to a close. Six years, six long years before my son's death, an overwhelming majority of the American people expressed by that vote that they wished no further involvement in the Vietnam War. If you interpret these young men who refused to serve in Vietnam as having abandoned America in her time of need, then I ask you—did you not yourselves, as the duly elected representatives subject to the will of the American people, by allowing that war to go on and on and on, abandon us in our time of need? What difference is there between a government which forces its dissidents to seek exile and a government which exiles its dissidents? Today, Canada, Sweden, and Europe, the world is filled with a generation of young American Solzhenitsyns. If I am to receive any comfort from my son's death, then let me believe that he died so that some other mother's son, somewhere, might now come home.

"Thank you."

When my testimony ended, Father Smith smiled and whispered in my ear, "And you pretended to be an amateur!"

A short period of discussion followed, during which I addressed the panel. "Why hadn't a senator, a congressman, a president, or an ambassador lost a son in Vietnam?" I asked. "Where did they come from, these citizen soldiers? They came from the farms in the Midwest, from the ghettos in the cities, and from the hills of West Virginia."

Congressman Henry Smith of New York said he had no sons to give but that a great number of senators and representatives had sent sons to fight in the war. I reminded him that over a ten-year period, only twenty-six of their sons had served in Vietnam. He insisted that my figures were not accurate nor was my statement true.

While lobbying that spring in Washington for the passage of S.B. 609 (a bipartisan "End the War" amendment sponsored by five senators, including Harold Hughes of Iowa), I had learned that every young man in Senator Hugh Scott's office had a conscientious-objector rating. I told the panel that the boys from the hills of West Virginia and Pennsylvania had never heard the term "CO."

Scott had been one of the strongest supporters of Nixon's Vietnam policies right up to the end. What I had learned from the Pennsylvania senator's staff strengthened my belief that those who supported Nixon to the fullest could avoid having to pay this terrible price.

As the hearings closed a young Jesuit priest emerged from the audience, ran to the podium, and demanded that Smith apologize to me. The congressman said with a smirk, "I was just shooting from the hip to make points while on camera."

Father Robert Drinan, a congressman from Massachusetts, came down from his place on the panel. He embraced me, saying, "Bless you, Mrs. Mullen, for coming." (I had met Drinan and visited with him at the 1972 National Democratic Convention in Miami.)

When I got up to leave the hearing room, I was approached by an ABC reporter. He took my hand and told me how sorry he was that I hadn't testified earlier. If I had been on before three o'clock his network would have carried my entire testimony. It was now five o'clock, and only a fraction of it would be shown. However, it appeared on the TV news that evening and was carried for a couple of days on the radio.

As I entered the hallway, a man identified himself as a television cameraman. Tears streamed down his face. He reached for my hand and said, "Thank you for coming, Mrs. Mullen. I lost my only son in Vietnam, never to be heard from again. And yesterday my wife presented me with a baby boy, twenty years after the birth of our first son." He was crying from both the pain of losing one son and the joy of gaining another. I could say nothing to him—only squeeze his hand in understanding.

Only three of the people who testified (out of forty-five) were quoted in *Newsweek* and *Time*, and I was one of them. I also gave a leading college textbook publisher permission to print the statement.

In 1976 President Carter granted unconditional amnesty to those who refused to serve, allowing the young men to return to their families.

# ELEVEN : MOTHERS AND VETERANS

The most poignant letters following our protests against the war came from the families of fallen servicemen. They didn't speak of their loved ones in heroic terms, nor did they express any pride that they had died 10,000 miles from the land they were sworn to protect. A common theme was "Why?" They had found no one able, or willing, to provide an answer.

In Peg and Gene Mullen, these bereaved families found kindred spirits. Here were two people who understood what it meant to spend hours in silent grieving over a son whose life was wasted in a winless war—a man that survives in memory as a small boy playing "cops and robbers."

My fury over Michael's needless sacrifice was boundless. I lashed out at everyone and everything. I participated in radio talk shows, made television appearances, and gave newspaper interviews throughout the Midwest. People listened.

Especially heartbreaking were the stories of families who had been ordered not to open the sealed caskets. Most didn't realize that morticians faced a federal penalty of $10,000 were they to break the seal. If the families had decided to open the casket themselves, however, who in the Defense Department would have known about it? Who would have reported it and to whom? Otherwise, these parents would never know for sure whom they had buried.

One woman wrote that the army told her her fiancé was killed in a firefight, that he shot two Viet Cong before an enemy bullet exploded the grenade on his belt. After two weeks of being listed as missing-in-action, his body was returned in a sealed casket. The survivors assistance officer told his family that his missing medals were on the uniform he was buried in. She would never know if the body was that of her fiancé—she believed his uniform was probably a body sack. In bitterness she remarked he had traded his life for a Bronze Star and a Purple Heart.

Another letter came from Ann Pine, a Gold Star mother:

> My son was listed as missing (first lie from the Defense Department)—yes, he died a hero saving his brothers for which they awarded him the Bronze Star.
>
> What the army didn't tell me was on Jan. 2, 1968 many of our soldiers in the 1st Air Cav were sent into an ambush. . . . Their bodies were left to rot in the sun for three to four weeks, saying they were sending out search parties and offering rewards. I noticed in the film the Army said the boy would have an escort, a friend from Vietnam, to accompany it. They only asked if I wanted his body back, or left in Vietnam.
>
> I never saw my son's body (a closed casket,) excuse was because of the black and blue marks, not the rot from being left there in the jungle. I didn't receive his personal belongings. For 11 years now I have been trying to see the President, tried to talk to the Army, senators and congressmen but have gotten nowhere. If I could only get a list of his buddies so someone could tell me what happened.
>
> No one understands—I'll never really know if that was my

> son's body in the casket—or just rocks! They refused to open the casket. Now, after nine years they tell me I could have seen his body—more lies.
>
> Please forgive my scrawl. I think I have met you at one of the demonstrations in Washington. I am one of the Gold Star mothers that threw her son's medal over the Capitol wall. The flag that covered his coffin is buried under a tree on the mall around the Capitol.

I don't remember meeting Ann when we marched in the antiwar moratorium in April 1971, but she was very visible in the publication called the *New Soldier*, a pictorial account of the entire week's events prepared and written by John Kerry and the Vietnam Veterans Against the War. When I met Kerry in D.C., I asked him to send me a copy of the book. It came to me with fly sheets filled with autographs. It is a vivid and startling memorial to Vietnam veterans and should be in all school libraries. Lieutenant Kerry was the first army officer to return from the war and address the Congress about the corruption of the war, pleading for its end. Today he is a U.S. senator from Massachusetts, involved in efforts to locate all missing soldiers.

Mothers, girlfriends, and sisters wrote in, many of them believing that Gene and I were "the lucky ones." Our son was killed, but his suffering was brief. He didn't come home a stranger or a "vegetable," as some wrote, bound to a bed or needing a wheelchair or doomed to spend the rest of his life in an institution.

This thought has occurred to me, particularly when I've taken calls from disturbed veterans at odd hours of the day or night. In their desperation, these men turn to strangers for help. I try to oblige, listening while they describe their torment and anguish, their struggle to make it through another day at work. My last such caller kept me on the phone from 2 to 5 A.M.—I was afraid to hang up on him. Over the years, I've asked each of these troubled vets to drop me a postcard so I'll know they're OK. But the postcards don't come, and I'm haunted for days after each call with the thought that the caller has chosen death.

Once I heard from a woman who had fallen in love with a veteran. She said her man had survived the war "statistically," only to die tragically in an auto accident "because his mind was so entangled with those vivid memories of war. Too vivid to forget." Her man "escaped using drugs." As a friend said, "he thought he could fly."

"I'm not ashamed of the fact that my husband served in the war," wrote the wife of a former machine gunner, "but it's not something I can feel good about. He still has nightmares, and he sometimes drinks heavy when it's on his mind, but he is a hard worker and a good father to our son."

A woman from Texas wrote that she, too, had a son named Michael who served in Vietnam. "I feel like I know you," she said. He was the youngest of her four children, whom she had raised by herself. She had taught him to fish and hunt, and they were very close.

Her son had returned home, she wrote, but when he came back he was addicted to drugs. "After five years of quitting, then starting again, he gave up and took an overdose to end the hell we all lived in. . . . It wasn't easy to part with our Mikey—we called him Mikey, too—but thank God, Peg, you did not have to stand by for five years, feeling so helpless, and watch your son destroy himself."

The drug abuse theme became all too familiar. No less common among returning Vietnam veterans were changes in mood and personality. Mental distress was a frequent carryover from the Vietnam experience, whether manifested as drug addiction or in a veteran's behavior.

Many people told us their sons had been reluctant participants in the war. An Iowa parent wrote that her son did not want to go. He had been drafted ahead of many others who were older, who she claimed never even had to go in for a physical. Nonetheless, he was sent to Vietnam, where he died in an ambush.

Not all of the young men, however, went to Vietnam against their will. An Iowa woman wrote that her son had been wounded and therefore did not have to return to Vietnam. But he chose to return and was killed three months later. Still, he went back to Vietnam believing that if he could help save even one life, it would all be worth it. She knew of other veterans who felt the same way, and she hoped I would find peace of mind.

This mother was truly blessed. How much easier it would have been for us to accept the death of our son in Vietnam if he had believed in the cause that took him to his death.

One woman sent along a clipping from the Mason City, Iowa,

*Globe Gazette*, which quoted from her son's last letter home, dated Christmas 1969, the day before his death.

> We just got back from the operation yesterday. It was a pretty rough one.
>
> This is supposed to be a cease-fire tonight, but we are going out on an ambush. Things are really screwed up over here. It is raining. The monsoon season is supposed to be getting over any time. (Earlier, he had written that he had been wet 30 straight days.) We are supposed to get a hot meal today. The rain is letting up a little so maybe the chopper will be able to bring it in after all. We won't know how to act, eating something besides C-Rations. (They hadn't had a hot meal, not even for Thanksgiving.)
>
> Looking forward to hearing what units the President is going to pull out of 'Nam. If it sounds like I'll be here my full year, I am going to take R and R with (wife) Nancy in Hawaii about June or July. It would be great for Nancy to do a little traveling.

At no time have I ever regretted my activities in opposition to the war. I was always confident of Gene's support. Michael's parting plea for me to "never stop" protesting has stayed with me throughout the years. The letters from veterans also offered support. Typical was a letter we received from a disabled veteran from Illinois:

> I do want you to know that it is people like yourselves who give me courage and make me want to live a full life. You give me hope.
>
> . . . I have to deal with the guilt I feel for having participated—but knowing that there are people like you who had the courage I didn't have to stand up against that horrendous war does help me. The emotional wounds are worse than the physical wounds, but with time, I hope that I can ease the guilt. I, frankly, will live with the anger.

The letters cheered us on, assured us that those who had experienced the war firsthand were on our side. Their message contrasted with what we were hearing locally, where we stood accused of profaning our son's memory, of bringing shame to our family, and neglecting our three college-age children. We held fast to the vets' support and found comfort in the fact that so much of it seemed to come from those who had suffered the most.

Though we lost Michael, we gained a host of adopted sons. We became a part of their slow rehabilitation—helping them make their way around the obstacles they faced on their return (often, these seemed more devastating than the jungles of Vietnam). Many needed only a few months to readjust to civilian life. Others found it more difficult, and still others failed miserably—succumbing to drugs or committing suicide. I've developed a daily habit of checking the obituary column in the local paper, and all too often I read of untimely deaths among men of Vietnam-era age.

In spite of denials by the Defense Department, I believe many veterans to be victims of Agent Orange and other powerful defoliants used by our troops in the jungle. Very few who tramped through those jungles have escaped the damage inflicted by the deadly chemicals. Often the infantry was actually sprayed with Agent Orange by confused pilots or those trying to dump unused chemicals before returning to base.

A short time ago, I contacted homeowners in my area of Brownsville to collect signatures on a petition calling for improvements to our streets. A young mother, with her four small children clinging to her, endorsed the petition. I asked whether her husband would be interested in signing. "I have no husband," she responded. "I buried him last week, totally eaten away from cancer—the result of Agent Orange." Only a few days before her husband's death, the courts had ruled against a class-action suit filed by Vietnam veterans who claimed they had been damaged by Agent Orange.

A young Vietnamese friend, Hong, living in Brownsville recently returned to her homeland to visit the family she hadn't seen for fifteen years. She described finding a great deal of "dead" soil, apparently contaminated, in areas around her mother's farm. Hong noticed that many of the infants were afflicted with open sores, although the polluted areas had been fenced off. She was positive that the skin afflictions were caused by Agent Orange. The babies didn't die but were ill for at least a year. No one knows what the future holds for these children.

Hong, who as a child survived the bombing of the Mekong Delta, is truly a veteran of the Vietnam War. She saw her father and his animals killed by a low-flying gunship as he worked in his rice fields. She sought shelter in nearby caves while American bombers dropped cluster bombs on their small farm, creating lake-size craters.

After the death of her father and a direct bombing hit of their home, Hong said, her mother took the young family to Saigon in order to survive.

One of the first veterans to contact us was Bobby, a young neighbor who had returned home after serving with the marines. He appeared to be well adjusted, but he needed a sympathetic ear. He began to drop by in the mornings, drink my coffee, and take up a lot of my time. Finally, I made the following suggestion: "I'll listen to you for an hour or two—and you can give me an hour or two of help with the yard." He agreed, and the arrangement proved advantageous for the both of us. Of course, when I followed him into the yard to help with the chores, the "talk therapy" continued.

Throughout his tour in Vietnam, I'd regularly inquired about him. His mother had been confident he wasn't in danger, since he had written and told her he was a dog handler. Since neither his mother nor I was familiar with the jargon of the war, we figured he'd been assigned to the kennels at base camp. When I asked Bobby about the job, he laughed. "Oh, sure, I handled dogs," he said, "one dog, which I led into the jungle ahead of my platoon while I depended on the dog to sniff out any trouble." These "point men" were expendable, and thousands of them died or were wounded by tripping booby traps.

Bobby and I became good friends, and he went on to make a life for himself in postwar America. He married and had a family but preferred the life-style of a rebel. He wore his hair long, cultivated a beard, and lived close to nature in a rural area.

Early on a June Saturday morning in 1970, we had a visit from a tall young black man. He walked into our kitchen like he had been there before and without hesitation greeted us as Peg and Gene. He didn't need to tell us that he was the Martin who had been in Michael's company and had written to us from Vietnam. He told us about Michael's last days in his company—how they became friends when Michael, learning that he, too, was from Iowa, had shared his *Des Moines Register* with him.

Although Martin insisted he was OK, one hour in his presence took its toll on us. He couldn't sit for more than a few seconds. He walked around the kitchen table incessantly, and every few minutes he went through the motions of shooting his enemy with an imaginary machine gun. Still, we continued to welcome Martin back to the farm and were there for him as he faced the challenges of an interracial marriage. Gene walked the bride down the aisle in her groom's church, where they were married by his father, a Baptist minister. Afterward, we hosted the reception at our farm home.

We supported the marriage but elicited a promise from Martin to allow their children to be baptized Catholic, the faith of the mother. As the babies arrived (four of them), they were presented for baptism as promised, and someone from the Mullen household was always available to be a godparent.

Martin has done well with his life, having attained an electrical journeyman's union card. His wife, Terry, has graduated from college with a degree in education, and their firstborn is in his senior year in engineering at Iowa State University. (Martin, the third, ranked second in the nation on his college entrance test scores in the field of engineering, and his schooling has been totally funded through various scholarships.)

Many of our contacts with veterans have been by telephone. Gene and I usually shared these calls. He tried to understand each caller's problems, but most left me uneasy—some of the disjointed conversations will stay with me forever.

Ten years ago I got a call at 2 A.M. from a young attorney in the Chicago area. When I asked if he realized what time it was, he replied, "I never know what time it is, and I don't have the slightest idea whether it's day or night." He went on to say he was sorry he hadn't called as soon as he returned stateside. He had been with Michael's company in Vietnam. Two days later I had a similar call from a veteran in Minneapolis. The call came during working hours. He described himself as an executive who wore a three-piece suit and carried an attaché case. I asked him why he was calling. "I force myself to come to work each day," he said, "and after two hours on the job I begin to panic."

I can only listen, but the really disturbed veteran needs more than I can offer. I often can't tell them where to get the help they need. So many have described bad experiences with veterans hospitals that I'm hesitant to send them there.

A call came one night in August of 1991 from a member of the U.S. Coast Guard, a former marine who had returned home after six months in the Pacific. He called during the night, disturbed—the conversation lasted three hours, during which time he would repeatedly hang up and call back.

He claimed to be the youngest Vietnam veteran in the country and said he had been in the service only a short time when the U.S. embassy fell. He said the marines were trampled by the masses of people trying to escape, resulting in the deaths of two.

The Vietnam syndrome is alive and flourishing, although the veterans have been home from Vietnam for fifteen to twenty-five years. During the summer of 1991 I was contacted by a veteran from the Boston area who was attending summer school in Iowa. He had originally phoned my son John to find out where I was living. John told him of my plans to come to Iowa in June and assured him that I would be happy to visit with him.

I'd been home a week when he called and asked me to meet him for lunch. He was about forty-five with graying hair, and as we enjoyed our food, he told me his story. He had been home from the war for two decades and had spent nearly seventeen of those years in bars—where he was drunk, drugged, and brawling—or in jail somewhere. As we talked I expressed my concern over the number of suicides among the returned veterans. He told me that Vietnam veterans' organizations were researching the problem, and many believed that more than 200,000 veterans had taken their own lives.

Finally, he was contacted by a veterans' religious group. He said he listened to them, and the result was a complete turnaround. He'd married and become the father of a beautiful baby daughter, and he was now positive that he would never again lose control of his life.

Then he told me the reason he had looked me up. While on combat duty more than twenty years ago, he'd been driving a jeep and hit a land mine. Four men riding with him were killed. Now, for the first time since his return, he felt he had the strength he needed to talk to the parents of the boys who died in his jeep. One of the victims had been an Iowa resident. He asked for my help in locating the family.

I spent several days making phone calls, and eventually I located the victim's grandmother. She lived near Des Moines, so I drove to see her. By the end of the week I was able to phone my new friend and give him all the information he was seeking. I had a feeling that when it came to actually meeting the family, however, he would probably back out. Recently, I placed a call to the grandmother and learned that the veteran had indeed driven several hours to spend a day with the parents of his dead comrade. They had taken him to their son's grave, and they appreciated his visit. They were not disturbed by his visit, as some in the family had feared.

My file of letters from veterans is a treasure trove. In tone and content they run the gamut—from deep sadness and bitterness to joy and satisfaction over having attained "the good life," through education, marriage, and beautiful children.

# TWELVE : FRIENDLY FIRE

In mid-April 1976 C. D. B. Bryan's book *Friendly Fire* was published. Michael Gartner, editor of the *Des Moines Register*, called to tell us he was interested in buying the rights to publish the story in serial form. We were sick at the thought of having our personal tragedy recounted in this statewide daily newspaper, so I pleaded with Gartner to reconsider. He was adamant, concerned that not enough people would read the book. "It is a story that has to be read," he insisted. We waited in anguish for the first issue.

Gene went off to work early on April 19. When he reached the John Deere plant, he sat down in the lunchroom for a cup of coffee and picked up the *Register*. The story was on the front page—all the heartaches revisited. How was he going to bear this? There was great animosity among his fellow workers over our stand against the war, and Gene was having trouble dealing with it. A large percentage of John Deere workers were veterans of World War II—they were proud of their service and proud of their uniforms. Most were members of the American Legion, and the legion supported the war. Gene's position on the war was likened to that of a "scab" during a union strike.

Gene's job involved making a final inspection of the tractors as they left the plant for delivery to dealers. That day, he found it necessary to "red-tag" (reject because of flaws) a great number of tractors, thereby angering both labor and management. By the time he arrived home, he was not feeling well. He planted two fruit trees in the front yard, but when he came in for dinner he was unable to eat. I called our son John, whose business was four miles away, and told him I was afraid his father was facing a heart attack.

John rushed over, and we left immediately for St. Francis Hospital in Waterloo, thirteen miles away. Passing cars right and left, he got us there in twenty minutes. Gene was able to walk into the emergency room. He was checked over thoroughly and cleared to go home. On the advice of an elderly doctor and friend, however, he was placed in intensive care for observation. About an hour later, Gene suffered a heart attack. He survived only because we had rushed him to the hospital. The attack was so massive he would have died at home.

Throughout Gene's stay in the hospital, the nurses cooperated in keeping the *Register* out of his room. Of course, publication of the story did not, in itself, cause his heart attack—it was the culmination of six years' grieving over the loss of his son. During this same period four fathers in the Waterloo area died suddenly after losing their sons in the Vietnam War.

The *Register*'s daily installments drew mail from farm wives to small-town doctors, lawyers, and teachers. The correspondents ranged from the fairly articulate to the unpracticed writer, but all seemed to regard Gene and me as two of their own. Because of our story, they'd realized that their state's contribution in human lives to the war was enormous and far out of proportion to other areas of the country. The military had always liked rural soldiers because, lacking sophistication, they were obedient and cooperative and not likely to create problems.

Gene spent three weeks in the hospital and was dismissed with a poor prognosis. His doctor told me he might live for six months. I don't know what he told my husband, but Gene had a habit of turning off his hearing aid in uncomfortable situations. His behavior during the next ten years was certainly not that of a man with a six-month life expectancy.

There's no question that, after Michael's tragic death, I became so preoccupied with the Vietnam War and the peace movement that those things seemed to dominate my life. No one realized it more than I. But it was that very preoccupation and sense of purpose that allowed me to carry on in spite of the pain.

The period in my life chronicled in *Friendly Fire* actually amounted to little more than one year—not the five years it took the author to write the book. My three surviving children were away at college during those months, and I was never aware of an estrangement from anyone in my family until I read Bryan's opinion in his unedited manuscript sent to me for approval. I'm sure I could have taken more time to listen to my children. We discussed Michael constantly but didn't talk about how each of us was dealing with his death.

Nevertheless, we remained in close touch. In the summer of 1970 Patricia and Mary held jobs and John attended summer school in Indiana. Patricia married in the fall, and I spent weeks working on her wedding. I made her wedding dress, along with dresses for the bridesmaids, and we held a reception at our farm home for seventy-five guests. I also spent several days in Iowa City helping decorate the newlyweds' tiny apartment.

During those years of turmoil, when college campuses across the country were alive with demonstrations, I kept close tabs on everyone. More than once, after hearing on the news that there would be a protest at the University of Iowa, I drove ninety miles to remind Patricia that she was in college to get a degree, not to get arrested in a demonstration. She often replied, "Mom, you do it. Why can't I?"

In the fall of 1976 Gene and I decided to seek a warmer climate for the winter, so we drove to Brownsville, Texas, in the Rio Grande Valley, a favorite retirement spot for Midwest factory workers and farmers. We'd visited there for six weeks in 1971 and had fallen in love with the balmy climate, the easy way of life, the Mexican culture, and, most of all, the proximity to the border. We moved to a mobile home court developed by a realtor, so we were fortunate to be living with a mixed group of neighbors. About half were winter visitors for five months and the remainder young Hispanic couples. We were only five miles from the International Bridge taking us into Mexico.

Bryan's book was being widely read, and through the gracious auspices of the postmaster in La Porte City, the mail it generated followed us. The phone calls also reached us, and we often were surprised by total strangers who'd been moved by *Friendly Fire.*

Two of the more memorable visitors during our first winter of retirement were a New Jersey couple. They'd traveled to Corpus Christi and on to South Padre Island for a week's vacation with one idea in mind—to meet Gene and Peg Mullen. After reading *Friendly Fire,* they had driven to our farm in Iowa to meet us. When learning that we had moved, they planned a trip to Padre Island near Brownsville. They wanted to talk to two people they believed would understand and help them. Their only child had returned from Vietnam, having served in the Americal Division, and had become a recluse in the mountains of southeastern Pennsylvania. If talking was the therapy they needed, we supplied it in abundance—a nonstop conversation for the entire week.

Another visitor was a Vietnam veteran from Iowa who had left his home, family, and job and taken to the road. Gene had read about the young man. His battle to recover his health and conquer his addiction to drugs after his return from combat had been featured in a publication of the John Deere Company. Gene had also known the young man's father, so he wrote him a long letter of support. The veteran left Iowa and came to the Rio Grande Valley to say good-bye to his parents (who wintered in the area) and then came to see us. We listened to him all afternoon, sympathized with him, but refrained from giving advice.

When the veteran got up to leave, we shook hands and asked if he had any plans. He looked up, his eyes filled with sorrow, and said, "I have no plans—I don't know where I'm going, only that I'll never come back."

During the winter of 1976/77 the John Deere Company removed Gene from medical leave, placed him on a permanent medical retirement, then followed up with the paperwork for him to go on Medical Social Security Retirement. From 1976 to 1979 Gene and I spent our winters in Brownsville, returning to Iowa each April to summer on the farm. It was a busy time, as there was much work to be done around the place—repairing and painting the buildings, maintaining a large lawn, and taking care of the fruit trees.

In the fall of 1979 John was married and continued to live at home with his bride. The following winter he asked if he could buy the homestead, and we happily sold it to him. In 1980 we spent the summer in Brownsville and found that we could tolerate the climate, so we made it our permanent residence.

We soon became acclimated to mobile home living. With only a small yard to maintain, we didn't miss the acres of lawn to mow or the orchard to trim and spray. It was easy to forget the rigors of farming and working off the farm: fighting the elements, shoveling snow, losing electrical power in a blizzard. We were finally able to relax. Gene and I missed our lifelong friends in Iowa, but we didn't feel lonely or isolated. We continued our daily walks to the mailbox and picked up cards and letters from total strangers.

In 1981 a man wrote to us from California:

> I read *Friendly Fire* about a year ago and it has taken me this long to decide if I should write or not. My friends have advised me to do so.
>
> I was in Vietnam from Jan. 23, 1969 through Jan. 17, 1970 . . . during the entire year I was in the Fire Direction Center (of Whiskey Battery, 3rd Battalion, 11th Marines) figuring data for 105mm howitzers. The reason for this letter is to let you know there is myself and, I'm sure, many others who see through the faulty conclusions presented in the book and the TV movie. These are:
>
> 1. No one was at fault. The error was a miscalculation in data.
> 2. You are parents overcome with grief, with little justification for your outrage.
>
> The author obviously had his own conclusions in mind before he even began the damn thing. Let me explain.
>
> First, gun data are given from the FDC to the guns only once. They are calculated and recalculated in the FDC and given to the guns with the guns repeating it back to assure accuracy.
>
> There is no correction or change in data until a forward observer has called in to the FDC. For this reason there could have

been no faulty data given or used between the first and second or any other of the following rounds. If the first round made it, all the following rounds must follow. Particularly with DT's (in the Marine Corps we called them H&I's) because the data are calculated and checked beforehand.

The only possible problem, given the information in the book, must have taken place on the guns. There are seven charges, or powder bags, used on a 105mm howitzer. The first is large and decrease in size up to seven. If the charge was seven and only six were put in, the round would fall short. This would be extremely easy to do if the people on the guns were drinking. The trajectory of the gun at anything but direct fire moves in a very high arc. Trees are not an excuse for anyone except someone knowing nothing about artillery.

The trajectory is always gradually up and quickly down. Mountains are calculated in mountainous areas, but never hills and certainly not trees. This excuse is asinine!

Second, given what I just said, I believe you were and are very justified in your anger. You have asked the right questions and gotten virtually no answers.

This may seem strange to you, I think not. But after 10 years I hold close to my heart the memory of my dead friends. . . .

I wish I could ignore that chapter in my life, but I am condemned to relive it, over and over. I'm alive now with one purpose—that is to see it does not happen again to your grandchildren, my children, or my children's children.

With love, one of your loving sons

Many letters like this one came to us over the years. One former World War II artillery officer actually wrote volumes on the subject for many months. Bryan had written it was just another unfortunate accident expected in the heat of battle. He explained that the height of the trees where the missile hit had not been considered in the original calculations. At no time did we think it was just another accident in the heat of battle; after all, there had been no activity in Michael's unit that night. We grieved a bit with each letter but felt we could do nothing. We hoped and prayed that someday, someone would tell us the true story.

Mary Crawford, a writer for *Ms.* magazine, first contacted us by telephone in late May 1976. Two weeks later her letter dated June 10 arrived:

> I've been thinking about our telephone conversation for two weeks. . . .
>
> One thing bothers me: in all the publicity, all the reviews, all the commentary on the book, your voice is not being heard. You are, after all, the center of this story. Your life has been profoundly changed. Your actions shaped the whole sequence of events. Yet the only picture we have of you as a person is Bryan's. And I have the feeling that he doesn't know you very well.
>
> One obvious example . . . is his consistent . . . playing down your lifelong political involvement. Another is his treatment of you as obsessed by Michael's death in some vaguely unhealthy way. I can't forget your comment that he views you as being "hatched" the day Michael died. . . .
>
> I couldn't help feeling drawn to you when we talked. Your life provides an example of enormous courage and integrity. Yet Bryan agrees with Schwarzkopf when he says that "what happened to the Mullens is an 'even more terrible thing' than Michael's death; they have become casualties of the war."
>
> You didn't seem like a casualty when I talked to you. On the contrary, you seemed like an articulate woman who could have a lot to say to other women.
>
> I would like to see the misconceptions about you and your family corrected. . . . We can give you a forum so that your values and the example of your life can reach other women, whose own lives may be changed as a result. I hope you'll think about what *Ms.* is trying to do, and reconsider your refusal. . . .
>
> Had I only read the book I would have had a very different picture of Peg Mullen. As it is, I feel privileged that our paths crossed, however briefly.
>
> Sincerely,
> Mary Crawford

I eventually relented—Crawford came to the farm and spent the day interviewing me. Her article appeared in the September 1976 issue of the magazine. I actually enjoyed having my story published in a feminist magazine. I had lessons on the subject from my mother.

In the early thirties she was Pocahontas County (Iowa) Democratic Chairwoman, many years before women generally held these kinds of positions. When my children were little, they loved to remind their father that he was married to a "liberated woman," and in one of his letters home, Michael wrote, "you are becoming more like Grandma with your politics."

In June 1976, two months after *Friendly Fire* was published, Courty Bryan made a special trip to see us for the purpose of obtaining permission to do a television screenplay. Gene was ill, recovering from his recent heart attack, so I visited with Courty alone. I told him that we would not grant him permission at that or any other time. We were still angry over Bryan's portrayal of (then) Colonel Norman Schwarzkopf, and we didn't agree with his having ended the story—our story—with a justification of the Vietnam War.

But Courty insisted he'd bring the story to television, even if it meant changing names and locale. He approached us later, this time by phone, but again we refused. Then there were more contacts from his agent and, finally, our first call from ABC-TV. A network official asked us to sign a release. I tried to make him understand that Gene had made little recovery from his heart attack and that we couldn't handle another invasion of our private lives. He told me I was probably the most miserable woman he had ever dealt with. I hung up on him.

We earnestly wished to avoid becoming the subject of another public exhibition. But we knew in our hearts we were powerless to stop it. We had forfeited our rights when we'd accepted Bryan's offer to write our story. He came to our home in April 1971 with credentials from the *New Yorker.* It was the plan of both the writer and the magazine to do a short story about us, to be published soon. We readily agreed—we felt that the people who read our story would join us in our struggle to end the war.

A month after Bryan contacted us about doing the screenplay, we received a long letter from a veteran who had lost a leg in the incident in which Michael died. He was pleading Bryan's case, citing many reasons why we should consent to the making of the film. The veteran wrote at length about his friendship with Michael—he told how they had traveled the jungle together for over three months and about the night Mike was killed. He then put in a special pitch for

Courty, reminding us that we couldn't expel the past from our minds no matter how hard we tried, for the past shaped our future. He mentioned that Bryan had put many years into bringing our story to the public, and he sincerely hoped we would reconsider our decision and allow the movie to be made. Of course, we resented Bryan's attempt to manipulate us through a veteran who'd "been there."

In October of the following year we received a letter from Fay Kanin, a well-known scriptwriter, asking if we would cooperate with her in the preparation of a television script. I informed her of our position. "We lived in anguish for five years while Bryan attempted to write the story," I said, "and when the manuscript reached us in September of 1975, we were appalled at what we read. It is our belief that, during the five years he worked on our story, it simply became his story, and we definitely did not like his version."

I explained that since the book came out, junior officers who were in Charlie Company when my son died had contacted us (and Bryan) to complain about his version of the story and his treatment of the military. I further advised her that Bryan himself had admitted to me—but not before the book was published—to having been conned by Schwarzkopf.

In short, I gave her all the reasons why we wouldn't cooperate. I told her we would soon be leaving Iowa for the winter and would be unavailable. I suggested that any further contact with the Mullen family be made through our daughter Patricia, an attorney in Muscatine, Iowa, at that time.

The entire family worried about the movie, which was being filmed despite our protests. We were concerned with what it was going to do to our lives. Finally, Patricia decided to file suit against ABC-TV on behalf of the three surviving children, alleging invasion of privacy. ABC responded by inviting the three plaintiffs to come to Los Angeles in September 1978 and sit in on the filming for a week. John and Patricia flew to California (Mary had a year-old baby and was unable to accompany them) and met many of the people involved with the filming of *Friendly Fire.* They were particularly charmed by Carol Burnett and eventually developed a warm relationship with Fay Kanin. At the urging of Patricia and John, we became friends with Fay and have corresponded over the years.

John and Patricia reported that the story was being handled well and said they believed that our family would not be harmed. They did insist on changes of the set representing our kitchen. After all, we had built a modern farm home in 1961, but the producers had followed Bryan's description and created a set resembling a home of the early 1900s. I still don't understand what that added to the film.

Meanwhile, Patricia's attorney in Muscatine followed through with the lawsuit. It was settled with a payment of $45,000, which was divided among Patricia, Mary, and John. ABC was thoughtful enough to ask whether we preferred that the production be aired while we were in Brownsville or at home on the farm. If shown in late April, as proposed, the fallout in Brownsville would have been minimal—all of our winter friends would have left the Rio Grande Valley to spend the summer at home. We agreed to April 22, 1979 (a Sunday), and arranged to stay in Texas.

A couple of hours before air time we talked to Carol Burnett. She was excited—there was reason to believe she'd win an Emmy for her effort. (The production, in fact, won a number of Emmys, but Carol's was not among them.) Gene and I debated about whether to watch the film (neither of us had read the published book). Personally, I knew I wouldn't be able to, but Gene was determined to sit through it. I worried about his having another heart attack, but there was nothing I could do.

I retired to our bedroom with a book and read throughout almost the entire telecast. At one point I emerged, but after two minutes of watching the film I began to tremble and had to leave the room. I have not attempted to view it since, although I did recently purchase a copy of the video for everyone in the family.

The flood of phone calls to our Iowa farm home began early, while the movie was being televised on the eastern airways. John and his wife, Jeanne, living in our home, were there to answer, having been prepared for an outpouring of support and sympathy. The calls didn't stop until the following Wednesday. They were computerized by Bell Telephone—as one caller hung up there was another waiting on the line.

A few days after the broadcast, I heard from a motelkeeper in southern Iowa who happened to have the same telephone number as ours, but with a different area code. She wrote: "You must have received hundreds of letters and phone calls after the show with Carol

Burnett Sunday night. We especially know about the phone calls, as we got about that many. . . . We have been getting [your] calls for about two years, then since Sunday night they have been constant. Don't get me wrong, we don't mind. I just thought you might be interested."

We returned to the farm in Iowa a week later. We were expecting lots of mail, but we hadn't given any thought to the tourists driving into our farmyard to visit with us in person. During our first week we had visitors from New York, Texas, and California. Friends in La Porte City told us of many tourists asking directions to Michael's grave. We were almost ready to run away, but the traffic slowed down finally, and the visitors became less of a problem. Some days letters arrived in bundles—on others, only one or two reached us. All of them were answered, and we contacted many of the writers by telephone.

We didn't allow the new publicity to disrupt our lives, though. We traveled for several weeks that summer, through the Black Hills and then on to visit Mary and her family in Montana. From there, we drove through Glacier National Park and north to Calgary, Alberta, Canada. We followed the beautiful Canadian Highway west to Vancouver. Close friends lived on Vancouver Island, and we spent several days in their home on the bluffs overlooking the Georgia Straits. I went fishing with our host and caught three large salmon. It was the first and only time I've fished for salmon. After a three-week trip we returned to the farm until time to make our October trek south to Texas. Again we fell into a daily routine of walking to the mailbox at 9:30, opening and reading the mail, and attempting to answer it.

A mother from Missouri let us know that we were not alone:

> I am sure you spoke for many thousands of families who have this feeling of anger and frustration which doesn't seem to go away with the years. We also had some of the same questions after our son's death, many not answered. We, too, talked most of the time about the war and our son's death, and many people were turned off by what we were saying, by our preoccupation with the war. Most of them said they were tired of hearing about it and seeing it daily on television. But our boys couldn't get away from it by turning off TV. They had to die to leave it.

A mother who had lost her son nine years earlier wrote:

> It took Charley and me nine months to make Chuck with God's help. It took the Vietnam War and the Marines just nine months to kill him. . . . I wish he had gone AWOL—I wish he had deserted—I wish I had broken his leg when he was last home. We love him so, and have to accept this.

A veteran from North Carolina corresponded with us in December 1978 after reading the book:

> I was drafted in November of 1966 and went to Vietnam. . . . But . . . I came back. I didn't want to be there. My mother pleaded for me not to go. My family even offered to finance a trip to Canada. Just so I wouldn't go to Vietnam. But I was too proud. Boy what a bunch of "Bullshit" that is now.
>
> I now am married and have a son who will be four in December. His name is "Michael"! . . . I love him dearly. I know that this might sound bad but should another Vietnam arise, God forbid, there is no way he will go. I don't know how I will handle it, but I know that he won't be there.

From Iowa, a nineteen-year-old wrote to us about her brother and the impact his death had upon her and her family:

> The last nine years have brought a lot of changes in our household. My dad lost his trucking business in 1971 because after Dennis' death he lost interest in everything and even the rest of the family. It was hard for me to understand then, but now I realize what the death of an oldest son can do to a father. They were very close.

Three months after the telecast of *Friendly Fire*, a supportive letter came from a woman from San Antonio, Texas. She wrote that the show and the book "hit at the gut emotions of Vietnam like nothing else has done so far." She added:

> I wish Vietnam never had been, to leave so much hurt and division in our country. It did happen and I hope to God our country never forgets what it did to our generation with its political policies and the apathy of so many Americans. . . .
>
> Thank you for not quietly accepting your son's death.

Many others also wrote to offer support, as in a letter from a woman in California: "You have saved countless young boys who may face a similar situation in the future. If the people who run this country in Washington have learned nothing from the Vietnam experience, and it is doubtful they have, the mothers and fathers of America have learned much." Or, as one veteran wrote us, "Michael, not John Wayne, is symbolic of America."

Not all the letters we got came from strangers. One of them, from the young wife of a coworker of Gene's at the John Deere plant, read, "The part about the medal brought tears to my eyes, and for the rest of the movie. We feel especially privileged that you cared enough to share that special medal with us and our little Sam."

The medal she referred to was one which had been part of Gene's spiritual life since it was given to him in 1934 by a young student from China whom he had befriended at Marquette University. Gene had given the medal to Michael as he left for Vietnam, and it was returned later with small items in his leather shaving kit. The only other time Gene parted with it was when he gave it to the letter-writer's family to hang on the cradle of Sam, their cancer-stricken little boy. Again, the medal came back to Gene when Sam died.

Tina Bourjaily, another longtime acquaintance, wrote, "It must have been strange to see yourself played by Carol Burnett. An odd bit of casting, I thought, until I saw what the comedienne's sense of timing could do to a serious, dramatic role." Over the years, Tina and I have kept in touch by telephone and mail. In 1992 while attending classes at the Iowa Writers' Workshop, I took time out to have lunch with her. I wanted to discuss with her that I was working on a memoir. When I started to talk about it, she interrupted and asked, "Why in the world are you putting yourself through the agony of another story?" I could only restate my belief that the real truth of Vietnam and some awful truths about war in general are contained in the mass of communications that came to us as the result of the book and movie.

# THIRTEEN : GENE

Gene's health began to fail rapidly in the spring of 1986, after he suffered three cardiac arrests the previous Christmas. He died July 16 at the age of seventy in the hospital in Brownsville.

Gene was born in 1916 to second-generation Irish parents in Waterloo, Iowa. The Mullen grandparents came from County Louth and the McDermotts from County Cork. Both grandfathers were uneducated and signed official documents by "making their mark," but they died wealthy landowners. Pat Mullen lived to be ninety-one in the house he built in 1872, where his ten children grew to adulthood. When he died in 1926, he left each child an eighty-acre farm.

Gene's maternal grandparents, the McDermotts, retired in Waterloo close enough to their grandson's home that on the way to school he would run in the front door, grab a handful of Grandma's cookies, and run out the back door. Gene had fond memories of sitting quietly in the corner of the kitchen on Sunday afternoons while the elderly immigrants in the Waterloo community sat around his grandfather's kitchen table, sipped Irish whiskey, and refought Ireland's Black and Tan uprising in the 1850s.

Like most young people who graduated from high school in the midthirties, Gene had little money to go on to college. However, he'd saved enough to enroll in Marquette University in Milwaukee and managed to stay almost two years before he had to drop out. He worked off and on at various jobs, working for the John Deere Company during their peak seasons until World War II.

Gene and I met in the elevator of the federal building in Waterloo in the spring of 1940. He was a friend of the woman I worked for, and his boss was a political friend of my mother. We were caught in the middle of two matchmakers who felt that two Irish Catholics would make a suitable pair. He was working for the Census Bureau, and I was employed by the district office of the Works Progress Administration, commonly known as the WPA. We were married on November 22, 1941, in Sacred Heart Church, Pocahontas, Iowa, two weeks before Pearl Harbor.

Draft notices were in the mail early in 1942, but Gene failed his physical because of deafness. The deafness was the result of a serious ear infection at the age of seventeen, before the time of antibiotics. He was able to enlist in the Iowa National Guard, however, and later that year was drafted into the army for "limited service" to serve as permanent personnel on stateside army posts. He spent five years in uniform as mess sergeant, dividing his time between Camp Dodge, Iowa, an induction center, and Fort Logan, Colorado, a separation center. Michael was born in Des Moines six months before we moved to Fort Logan.

Gene had obtained the rank of master sergeant at the time of his discharge, as head of the enlisted men's mess hall. It was a difficult assignment—sometimes feeding two thousand soldiers on two or three hours' notice. Troop trains from the West Coast would pull into the fort at any time of day or night, loaded with soldiers to be discharged. General John Murphy, commander of the post, bragged

*Gene at Camp Dodge, Iowa, 1943.*

that Sergeant Mullen ran the best mess in the service. When General Eisenhower inspected the post in the summer of 1945, he elected to eat in the general mess with the enlisted men.

Prospects for employment and houses were bleak when Gene left the service in April of 1946. Neither of us had jobs waiting for us. His mother suggested we move to the family farm, and we did. Life on the farm turned out to be a terrible struggle. The land had been abused for years and would not provide a living for Gene's family, nor for his parents who had no other income. During this period both the John Deere Company and Rath Packing in Waterloo offered work to farmers during the winter months. This proved to be a boon to the many GIs returning to the farms. These part-time jobs eventually led to full-time positions, with wonderful benefits. For years Gene referred to the Deere Company as "St. John Deere."

Full-time employment off the farm enabled Gene to forge ahead in rebuilding the farm, which we bought from his folks in 1948. In making the purchase he obtained title to the first 120 acres in Pat Mullen's estate, homesteaded in 1852 by Mullen's father-in-law, John Dobshire. Often working sixteen-hour days, he was relentless in making improvements, to the dismay of his wife and children, who watched new outbuildings go up while living in Dobshire's original house. In 1961 Gene was able to build a new home, drawing his own plans. It became a showplace, built for parties, and we had lots of them. Gene loved to cook and was a great host.

At the time Michael was killed in Vietnam, life had become much easier for Gene. The farm was at top production of corn and soybean yields, and he raised three hundred head of hogs per year and fed twenty-five or thirty head of beef cattle. There was money in the bank, and his four children were excelling in high school and college. The responsibility of supporting his parents had ended upon their deaths in 1960. He earned six weeks' vacation on the job at Deere, enabling us to travel at least one month each year.

However, nothing had prepared him for burying his son. So, for the most part, Gene lived quietly with his grief—there was no release until the moment he died. He couldn't talk about it without finding himself in a rage—it was much easier to remain quiet.

In the early seventies Gene rented his land on shares and cut back his cattle and hog operation. He felt that renting on shares was the only equitable way to operate, enabling the renter to share equally with the owner, in good years and bad. When he retired after his heart attack in 1976, he was ready to enjoy life. He simply put out of mind the doctor's prognosis that, if lucky, he might live for three or four months. He always found it convenient to turn off his hearing aid when facing bad news. He lived life to the fullest for ten years in Brownsville—spending his days on a red moped, wheeling in and out of RV parks, meeting people from all over the country. At least once a week he brought strangers home to dinner, many of them becoming lasting friends. Unfortunately, the moped also gave him the opportunity to sneak the forbidden cigarette.

Among the local Hispanics, especially the young people, he was known as Mr. Amigo. He was always ready to pump up a bicycle tire or, if necessary, put a patch on it. He spent hours with our Mexican neighbor teaching her to speak English to enable her to find a job. At Christmastime in 1983 we enjoyed three weeks with friends at their hacienda in the mountains south of Mexico City. He passed the days roaming through the open market, spending five or ten cents at each stall. He didn't speak a word of Spanish, but that didn't prevent him from trying to teach his new Mexican friends his language. When our hosts would return later to their hacienda, the local people would inquire about "Señor Guapo" (Mr. Handsome). He loved everything about Mexico and would have retired there if he hadn't had a heart attack.

In Brownsville he was an easy mark for someone in a financial bind—many times it was done with a signed note from the borrower, for others it was a handout. He believed all his life that a handout came back twofold. Patricia recalls that one Christmas when she was small, he announced that for the Mullen family Christmas he had bought a new heating stove for a family in La Porte City who had no heat.

During the winter months of these retirement years we made many trips to the interior of Mexico. The highlight of these trips for Gene was a visit to the Shrine of Guadalupe in Mexico City. We attended mass there on Christmas Eve in 1983. During the summer months we returned to Iowa to visit John and Patricia and spent the rest of the summer traveling. Many trips were made to visit Mary and her family in Kalispell, Montana, with stops in Spokane to visit a niece. While eating dinner one evening with Mary Ann and her family, her young son Bill looked up at Gene and said: "This is the first time I've ever seen a man with an antenna in his head." (He was, of course, referring to Gene's hearing aid.)

Gene lived to see the birth of four grandchildren. He didn't worry about their births or whether it was a boy or a girl, he just prayed the name would be "Irish." Everyone cooperated—the first four were

*Gene in the living room of our farm home, 1980.*

named Ryan, Megan, Kate, and Kellee. Patrick Michael Mullen arrived a year after his grandfather's death.

Gene was buried in the old cemetery at Eagle Center, Iowa, next to Michael and our infant son, Daniel, who died two days after birth. The country church was overflowing, and this time we had no difficulties with the arrangements. The minister from the nearby Church of the Brethren graciously agreed to sing Gene's favorite hymns, "Ave Maria" and "How Great Thou Art." As a final tribute to a man who never forgot his Irish heritage, the soloist sang with gusto another favorite—"When Irish Eyes Are Smiling." It echoed throughout the church and cemetery as everyone made the slow, short walk to the grave site. My sister-in-law remarked later, "Peg, I didn't know whether to applaud or to cry."

In tribute to Gene's lifelong interest in American Indian history, his nephew Bill sent me a copy of Chief Seattle's famous speech. It begins:

> Do not stand at my grave and weep,
> I am not there, I do not sleep.

These words were engraved on Gene's tombstone.

The family received many mass cards and cash memorials, but one letter touched all of us. A young man who grew up as a neighbor had attended the funeral, and later that evening he wrote:

> Peg, it was good seeing you and your family again after all these years. . . .
>
> I remember the help Gene and Mike gave me in 4-H, though I wasn't a very good "4H-er." Patricia's intelligence used to frustrate me to no end in elementary school. I now appreciate her for making me try that much harder. . . .
>
> Mom and Dad both told me of your kindness and help you and Gene provided them when they were first married. . . .
>
> I will always be indebted to you for the largest single influence in my life, my observance of your family's perseverance in search of the truth following Michael's death. The blind patriotism and unquestioning obedience which had characterized this country before Vietnam were put behind us because of the efforts of Gene and yourself and others like you. My own loss of innocence and maturity/growth came about due to your efforts. . . .

I also need to thank you for helping me re-establish my relationship with Dad. It was through discussions of your efforts that Dad and I once again became father and son. . . .

Gene was a good man who accomplished great things. He will be missed by many.

I named my third son Michael.

Love,
Rick

In August of 1989 I had to vacate my home in Brownsville because of hurricane warnings. I'd been gone two weeks, and when I returned I found there had been a break-in. While sitting on the bedroom floor trying to sort out the clutter, I came across a sealed envelope marked "Do not open" in Gene's handwriting. Of course, I opened it.

Michael E. Mullen, born September 11, 1944, killed February 18, 1970. He was my son, my projection to the future. Each era of his life was a period of determination, each day a challenge.

Michael, when young, was small in stature, but never too small to help his father on the farm, nor his mother as an extra hand. When he served mass on Sunday his chin was level with the altar and his dark complexion projected from the white background of his surplice and cossack he wore.

He had a nickname so dear to me, "Joe Blow."

Do you remember, Mike, how determined you were in your 4-H projects, your friendly competition with your competitors? You did well, Son.

Then in high school your time was consumed with books, basketball and class plays; each year was a stepping stone toward your goal in life. How proud were your mother and father when you were awarded a scholarship to college.

You never had a vacation, did you, Son? The summer months during your college days you always worked, and on weekends you helped on the farm. The little time that you called your own, your hands were at rest but your mind was planning your future.

You graduated from college with honors, was offered and you accepted a Fellowship in Bio Chemistry, your educational field and your way of life.

You did not finish your education working for your Doctorate; someone, so small, so minute, but with the authority of life and death, said that you would do more good for your country by killing, than by feeding the hungry.

When you were home the 21 days before leaving for Vietnam you lived your whole life over again. You worked at every conceivable task you had ever done. Even to the last day, it was 10:30 at night when you came up from the fields. You must have figured that your life at home was completed. Something told you that you would never again walk the land that you so loved.

The expression, the last look on your face as you bade your father and mother goodbye; the show of strength in telling us that you would be alright and your wish that we would not stay to say goodbye when you boarded the plane. Michael, I will live with this til we meet again.

The letters you wrote home telling your mother not to worry, your persistent statements of the destruction, corruption and the unnecessary taking of human life, and finally, the order to finish the task of Search and Destroy on a village that the artillery had pounded for 3½ hours during the night. What was left, you and your men had to dispose of. I could not believe that this was my son, that this was what I had brought you into the world for. The taking of another life was not the voice of your conscience, but the dutiful acceptance in your role of a soldier. It was not because you justified the war or the political means to its end, but because you were, Mike, obedient and respectful, to what you were told to do.

I have remained silent til now, Mike. Your mother, in her own right, has grieved and protested your loss.

I, as your father now ask, "Who killed you, Mike?" Yes, I'm asking "Who killed you?" You never knew that night that you and your buddy were destined to die, nor the seven other casualties. How could you know, Michael, because you were asleep. I have not and will not accept the military definition of the cause that killed you. Why? Son, because your friends who were left, told us in writing and in conversation when they came home, of rumors of what happened that night. From the black medic who sat at your side and tried, in vain, to help you, from the soul brother with whom you shared your newspaper, from the GI on guard that was near you, from the Platoon Sgt. from Company C. They all told of rumors that they want answered. Are the rumors true, Mike, only you know now? Was it negligence of command by the officers in charge of the supporting artillery unit on Hill 410? Were they on duty under the influence of liquor and is it true that the artillery piece that killed you had a record of malfunction and it had killed others before?

If this be the truth then you died for no cause in this conflict with no definition. If there be justice in the minds of man, then man has not as yet lived as man.

Good night, Son

# FOURTEEN : A NEW WAR

Early in February 1990 a young reporter, Larry Fruhling, called me from Des Moines and asked if he could come to Texas and write a feature story on "What Peg Mullen Is Doing Twenty Years Later." I sighed and replied, "Larry, people in Iowa are happy I faded away, and I'm sure they don't want to hear about me today." He disagreed, remarking that he had been to La Porte City, my former home, where he'd spent some time with the townspeople and found them receptive to a story. He stopped to see my son John at his place of business and was assured that he would be welcomed to my home in Texas. As he prepared to drive away, John said, "You'll find my mother has changed little."

*At my home in Brownsville, Texas, 1990. The* Des Moines Register *ran this photo with their feature article on the twentieth anniversary of Michael's death. Photo by Larry Fruhling, reprinted with permission of the* Des Moines Register.

I relented, and Larry Fruhling came and spent almost five days with me. We talked and talked, laughed a lot, and he took pictures. I drove him to Mexico to walk through the markets—a great experience for the reporter who told me that he'd never been in a foreign country. We ate goat roasted on a spit, with tortillas and hot sauce, washed down with cold Mexican beer.

Larry later sent me a copy of his feature story on page one of the

*Des Moines Register*, dated February 18, 1990, the twentieth anniversary of Michael's death. I like the story, and it was a relief to find the accompanying photograph flattering. It has been a standing joke in my family that my face ruins all the group pictures.

The *Register* story resulted in the following letter—probably the most beautiful I received in the twenty years of mail since Michael's death.

> Dear Peg:
>
> This morning's well-written *Register* story prompts this long overdue letter of apology for some particularly boorish behavior on my part twenty years ago.
>
> I was a reporter at KCRG-TV when you launched your protests, in Michael's name, against the Vietnam war. I had returned from Vietnam in July, 1969, and returned to KCRG in January of 1970. I have read—and seen—*Friendly Fire.* And if I wasn't the reporter who so insensitively questioned your motives, I might just as well have been. I don't remember the exact dialogue, but it was something on the order of "Well, lots of mothers are in your place, they're not doing what you're doing." I also seem to recall my saying something to the effect that "I have just come back and I don't think it's an unjust war."
>
> Over the years, I've thought about how stupid, young, naive, and downright dumb I was not to understand the source of your pain and why you were fighting as hard as you did against that inane war.
>
> So, I seek forgiveness.
>
> I keep a rubbing of Michael's name taken from the memorial in Washington in front of my desk as a constant reminder of my insensitivity.
>
> More important, I suppose, is the fact that having read and seen both *Platoon* and *Born on the Fourth of July*, I've come to realize how right you were in 1970 and, judging from this morning's paper, how right you continue to be.
>
> I have come, in the years since I returned from Vietnam, to be appalled by the folly of that war in particular, and other wars in general. I've also developed quite a lot of disgust for this or any nation that applauds while purposefully turning its finest young men into inhumane beings.

I recall seeing *Platoon* and being—oh, I don't know, disgusted, revolted, appalled, shocked or maybe all of those emotions at once—as the audience—mostly youngsters—cheered cinematic acts of inhumanity much as they might have cheered on Rambo. To them, *Platoon* was a "movie."

To me, in those parts which I was familiar with, it was a replay of my mind's memories—frame by frame. There were several of us older folks, obviously veterans, in the audience who were stunned by the impact of the film on this younger generation.

My mother taught me that words, once spoken, can never be recalled. I wish it were not so; I would recall mine spoken to you at your home—so like the one I grew up in—near La Porte City as we sat in the kitchen and talked.

Perhaps my belated realization of my ill behavior and this too inconsequential attempt at apology will make no difference—I have not yet learned hurt—but I think of you often; I will, for the rest of my life, honor Michael's memory and that of his mother, father (for I remember Gene, too), and his family.

Furthermore, Peg, I am now of an age where I (long after most others, I expect) have come to really, truly, understand what you were doing. My own son is almost 18; I expect that your most lasting legacy will be that of role model for those of us who must now face the all too real possibility of losing our own sons, too.

We, however, thanks to you (and thanks, too, I expect to Oliver Stone and Ron Kovic and the other tale tellers) know how to fight before it's too late.

The *Register* article was wonderful and inspiring. And it gave me a chance to write. Thanks for reading this; I also want to express my far too belated sympathy about Gene.

God bless you, and please keep up the fight. It is worth it.

The story in the *Register* also brought a telephone call from Peg Burke of the Physical Education Department, University of Iowa, asking if I would speak at a seminar in July entitled "Women Leaders in Peace and Justice." I accepted without much thought.

In April I received a formal invitation requesting a copy of my speech. I was informed that there would be an honorarium, that I would have two hours' time, and that I would be the keynoter on

Friday evening. I called Peg to say, "I do not write speeches, I pay people to listen to me." Then I asked if she had gotten the wrong Peg. She assured me I could handle it and that there had been no mistake. She said she wasn't too concerned with having a copy of a prepared speech, adding, "We know you can talk!"

I drove to Iowa for the summer from my home in Texas, stopped in Des Moines to visit Patricia for a day, and then proceeded to Iowa City. The seminar's organizers sent a driver to pick me up at my hotel, since I didn't know my way around the university. When we reached the building where the seminar was being held, I was met and greeted by several women who treated me like an old friend.

When it was time for me to speak, I approached the stage carefully because I was wearing heels, brought out of the closet for the occasion. I had managed three steps toward the platform when suddenly I caught a heel and fell flat on my face. I got up, approached the dais, and addressed the audience. "Most of you know me because of Carol Burnett's portrayal of Peg Mullen—she has made a living doing pratfalls, and why can't I?" Kicking off my shoes, I began by explaining why I had decided to speak out again after a decade of silence. The reason, I said, was that the commander most likely to lead the U.S. military into the next war was someone who frightened me. The man, Norman Schwarzkopf, was my late son's commanding officer in Vietnam.

I spent thirty minutes relating some incidents I had read about, together with tales told me by bitter ex-GIs. I vented twenty years of dislike for a man who, in my eyes, stood only for war—a man who would win promotion and advancement because of his ability to wage war. "What kind of man is this?" I asked my audience. "Decisions he made as commanding officer resulted in the slaughter of beautiful young men, many with goals far nobler than his. Thousands of young soldiers, and their dreams, were sacrificed in a cause the entire world now recognizes was unjust.

"What kind of man is this?"

What my audience and I did not know was that within a few short months my "colonel" would be introduced to television viewers throughout the world as "Stormin' Norman" Schwarzkopf, that we'd have to endure months of selling-the-general by the media, or that we'd hear him described as a "teddy bear," a lovable individual whose eyes would brim with tears at the mere mention of his beloved troops—and oh how he loved his boys.

At times I have questioned my own feelings about Schwarzkopf. Can it be that I've made him into a monster because I needed someone to blame for Michael's death? Of course, I realized years ago that the colonel was merely following orders in his mindless pursuit of body count in Vietnam, but I won't forgive his having allowed the sacrifice of so many young men, most of them draftees, in a cause he had to have known was futile.

When I returned to Texas in early September, I found inquiries from the *Nation* and *Progressive* magazines, both wanting interviews. Then to my horror, I learned my July speech in Iowa City had been aired on National Public Radio.

For the next five months I felt like I was under siege, and I had to leave home to find a little peace. I installed an answering machine, and, for the first time in my life, I disconnected the telephone in the evenings. It seemed every reporter wanted to know more about the general.

I was grateful to have close friends in Brownsville who were in agreement with me that the war was the result of President Bush's personal feud with Saddam Hussein of Iraq. We were angry, but there were too few of us. There was no doubt that Desert Storm took over my life during those months. Several of us organized to march each Saturday morning in front of the Brownsville post office. Some mornings only fifteen came, and only once did we draw as many as seventy-five. Our spirits soared the few times that Bishop John FitzPatrick joined us. This type of activity was new to Brownsville, and there was little response from the people who drove in and out of the post office parking lot. After several weeks, one young woman joined us with a sign reading: "Honk if you agree with us." The response was immediate—the honks were a symphony to our ears, and we cheered.

I was asked to speak at a local private high school on the subject of war, particularly the Gulf War. It wasn't until I arrived that I learned I would be debating the commander of the local VFW. He was a very attractive forty-five-year-old Hispanic, bedecked with medals earned in the Vietnam theater and a hero in the eyes of the Hispanic students. He graciously suggested that I make the first statement, but after only a few words into my talk I realized that I was being cast in the role of "the enemy." When I finished, the veteran rose in rebuttal, and we sparred for a half hour before opening the floor for questions and comments.

A student spoke up: "Mrs. Mullen, you are bashing the president, and you have no right to do that."

"Are you familiar with the Constitution?" I asked him. "Young man, it is my right, and I've been bashing presidents since I was eighteen."

His response chilled me: "Mrs. Mullen, President Bush is our leader, and if he commands us to go to war, we obey. And in our culture women do not have opinions, and if by chance they do have opinions, they remain silent."

I felt I was losing the battle but had to make another try at reaching their minds. I discussed the reasons Bush had given for going to war, reminding them that early on it was "to protect our way of life." I asked them to think about whose way of life was at stake.

"Is it your way of life, with three cars in the garage, your father driving a Mercedes, your mother a Lincoln Town Car, while you drive your own sports car into the school parking lot?" I asked. "Or is it the life of 90 percent of the inhabitants in the Valley, the homes that supplied the troops in the desert?" I reminded them of the poverty and hunger that put many of these young men and women in uniform. "They are in the service," I said, "to better their own way of life—not to protect the three-car garage." I pulled out all the stops and suggested that while they were eating dinner that evening they ask their parents, "Mom and Dad, would you give up one car for the duration to save a life in the desert?"

The teacher of the class dropped over to see me the next evening and told me that I had left the students very angry. But a few weeks later, after the war vote was actually taken in the Senate, he told me that the class was polled and a majority of the students now opposed the war.

By December the elderly Mothers for Peace were calling each other from east to west, north to south, all of us appalled that our years of struggle for peace had come to naught. Most of us were old and tired and couldn't face another round of protests like those of the sixties and seventies.

By January of 1991 I was in touch once more with Mary McGrory of the *Washington Post*, a correspondent who had befriended me back then. We needed to discuss our personal feelings about the mood of the country—we both found it difficult to understand the war fever that was apparently sweeping the country, and we wondered where the active peace movement had failed. Mary would encourage me to come to D.C. and march, only to call back a few days later and tell me not to come.

Meanwhile, I made up my mind to go anyway. I placed an ad in the *Brownsville Herald* inviting participation and giving the date and time for departure of the bus as well as the cost per passenger. It was up and down for the next ten days, but by departure time we had a load of thirty-eight. There were a few students, relatives of some who were serving in the Gulf War, and at least four mothers who had never traveled outside the Rio Grande Valley.

We left Brownsville early Thursday morning. Our thirty-eight-hour trip through the southern states was long and tedious, and we were continually cautioned by the bus drivers not to mention our destination during any of our stops. I'm sure we would have provoked violence had we carried signs on the bus or discussed the futility of war during a meal at one of the truck stops.

We arrived in Washington shortly after midnight and knocked on the door of the Unitarian church in the heart of the city. The door was opened by Mary McGrory's secretary, Tina, who had been waiting for us. She greeted us warmly and apologized for lack of space in the church basement. She said that busload after busload had shown up and that no one had been turned away. Tina said it seemed to her that the entire state of Minnesota had showed up to march in support of newly elected senator Paul Wellstone, a leading opponent of the war.

The floor where we were to rest was already covered with a sea of bodies—it reminded me of sardines in a can, but each of us managed to find a space to sleep. I spread my coat and blanket on a bare spot where, except for an awareness of someone's feet in my face, I managed to sleep for the next five hours.

We were told we must vacate the church basement by 8:30 in the morning, because the street people would be in for breakfast. We ate at a nearby McDonald's and boarded our bus for a short ride to the parade staging grounds. We parked in the street and were met by a police officer who told us we could leave the bus there. A few days before we left Brownsville, parade instructions had been mailed to us telling the bus drivers to proceed to RFK Stadium after unloading passengers. The police officer beckoned us to gather around while he gave instructions for the march. He cautioned us to be peaceful, as orders had been issued to arrest 40,000 that day. All I could think of was that the paranoia of the Nixon years never seemed to go away.

The march was massive but orderly, and the only police I saw that afternoon were the ones standing elbow-to-elbow around the White House. Dan Rather and Diane Sawyer described us on the news that evening as "old hippies" from the sixties and put the number of marchers at 40,000. It was great to see all the seniors, many in wheelchairs, who turned out for the march. As I walked along with my sign, "Abuelas for Peace" (Grandmothers for Peace), I was approached by a tall slender man in the New York group who said, "Everyone on the street wants to know if the little old lady from the Rio Grande Valley got here."

I showed him my sign in Spanish, saying, "I'm not as old as Mary McGrory wrote in her column yesterday. I'm not the little old lady from Dubuque in tennis shoes, but here I am, and I must look ninety today." The lanky, elderly New Yorker took off down the street, shouting: "She got here, she got here." As we walked along, a CBS reporter started coming toward me and Lupita, who had accompanied me from the Valley. I suggested that he interview my young friend, as she had a brother in the desert. He wasn't interested, but when the CNN reporter approached us, he jumped at the chance. Lupita, a beautiful Hispanic woman, looked directly into the camera and said in Spanish, "This is the only way I know to save my brother from death in the Gulf." Her family was overjoyed when they saw and heard her on cable TV that evening.

After the marching was over, we listened to an array of speakers, but the passion of the anti-Vietnam War days just wasn't there. A war had started, but no one in the country gave a damn, except, perhaps, the families of those who were to fight and die.

When the speakers had finished and the demonstration was over, we walked a short distance to our bus and climbed aboard for our return trip south. The driver said he regretted that we weren't staying over a day so that he could give us a tour of the capital. As we were leaving the city, he pointed out everything of interest that could be seen from the bus. I had my first glimpse of the Vietnam Veterans Memorial.

We drove into Brownsville early Monday morning, just as most people were on their way to work or school. The little old lady from the Valley went home, hung a "Do Not Disturb" sign on her front doorknob, and took to her bed for two days. Later, I told my nephew, who lives nearby, that I would never engage in another antiwar protest. "Oh, I think you will," he replied. "You'll be in a nursing home, organizing the occupants, leading them down the halls in their wheelchairs, beating on bedpans for peace."

Marching in Washington did nothing to ease my anguish over the Gulf War. It was in full swing—it devoured nearly twenty-four hours a day of television network time and was on virtually every station. It was inescapable, and we were a captive audience. At least once each day we were treated to a segment on General Schwarzkopf himself. There he was, smiling, in his desert fatigues, getting all misty-eyed while speaking of his boys.

Did he remember his boys from Vietnam, I wondered. How about all the dead, the legless, the mindless, the druggies? Did he think of them and their seemingly endless days and nights of horror as he pinned on his four stars each morning?

Did he recall his obsession with body count, the very key to his advancement and promotion during and after that undeclared war? Was there not the least remembrance of those who died from friendly fire?

For twenty years I had prayed that the horror of Vietnam would remain so much with us that it would, indeed, mean the end of all wars. But bombing in the Gulf War began on the exact date chosen many months in advance by the president, even though the most informed people in the U.S., both in and out of government and the Pentagon, testified day after day for weeks in Congress against the advisability of going to war in the Middle East. Before long, editorial cartoonists and other critics were sarcastically referring to the Gulf War as one of President Bush's "thousand points of light."

Most Americans cheered, waved flags, tied yellow ribbons around lampposts, and watched the high-tech war unfold from the comfort of their living rooms. "We're finished with the Vietnam syndrome," seemed to be the message. "Our country is back on target. Patriotism is alive once again. We can annihilate anyone—yes, anyone—who doesn't agree with us."

The few of us who chose to be in the minority found ourselves alone. Searching for ways to protest, I put all flag postage stamps upside down on the letters I mailed and displayed a small flag upside down in my front window. Each morning I would tie a batch of green ribbon bows and pin them on my dress when I went shopping. Clerks and checkout men and women were always curious, and I would tell them the green bows stood for peace and without hesitation pin one on them.

The selling of the general continued. Every evening Dan Rather or Peter Jennings appeared live in the desert with the man who appeared destined to become a national hero.

Then it happened. On the morning of February 1 the television networks were abuzz with a news story. Newspaper headlines announced: "Eleven Marines Die in Desert by Friendly Fire."

Tragic mistakes of Vietnam, Grenada, and Panama were being repeated. General Schwarzkopf had been second in command in the Grenada invasion and became involved in a friendly fire situation when one member of his headquarters company was killed and fifteen were wounded. His command post on the beach, at the time of the invasion, had not been marked with a smoke flare like other areas housing friendly troops, resulting in an air attack called in by a marine officer.

After the Gulf story broke, a very sober General Schwarzkopf faced the cameras and was besieged by reporters wanting details. Hadn't he been involved in such an episode previously, someone asked. "Stormin' Norman" bristled and replied, "I've been under friendly fire, but I haven't complained about it for years like some have." Another questioner wanted him to discuss an old theme from the Vietnam days, body count. The general sidestepped that question. Someone else asked why the marines had been sent into enemy territory even though the president had not yet declared the start of the ground war. Without hesitation Schwarzkopf said, "We were just goosing the enemy."

I was trembling. I waited in vain for just one reporter to ask, "Why was it necessary to 'goose' the enemy?" The result: eleven marines were dead, the first of the "acceptable casualties" so glibly voiced by the proponents of the war. "How acceptable," I asked myself, "to the loved ones left behind?" Now, with the newscasts full of stories relating the marines' deaths, I thought of Lupita who had marched with me in D.C. Her brother, Oscar, was in the area that had been hit. For the next twenty-four hours I agonized over this.

Late on the day after the tragedy, Lupita came to my door in tears. She said Oscar had called home to report that he was the sole surviving marine on his troop carrier. He told of the men's panic when they spotted the American bombers—how they jumped from their vehicle, throwing everything at hand into the air in a vain effort to alert the pilots. The marines were screaming for their lives as their own men swooped down on them with that same destructive firepower that the Pentagon extolled every evening on the nightly news. There'd been no last-minute effort to abort the bombing.

"Oscar remembered reciting the 23rd Psalm," Lupita told me, "and as he said it, something seemed to cover him—he described it as a shroud. A few seconds later he became aware of his surroundings and looked around to see the young driver of his carrier minus a shoulder and arm—dead bodies all around."

Within a few hours of the report of the friendly fire incident, I received an invitation to appear live on NBC's *Today* show the next morning. I said I would appear, but when the producers asked that I travel to San Antonio or Dallas, I said to them, "I'm retired in Brownsville, and if you want to interview me you'll have to come here." They agreed, and later that afternoon I received a call from a gentleman wanting my address and saying, "Mrs. Mullen, I have been hired to carry you to the NBC studio in Brownsville in my limo tomorrow morning."

I live about a mile from NBC's affiliate station in Brownsville, while the caller was located in McAllen, sixty-five miles away at the other end of the Valley. I laughed and declined his offer of transportation, explaining that I could certainly get there on my own. He phoned back two hours later, saying, "Mrs. Mullen, this is José. Please let me pick you up—I have been eating beans and rice all winter and I desperately need this job." "José," I said, "you have the job, and I don't mind if you drive five hundred miles to pick me up."

I'm sure when the limousine arrived, José had to back into our narrow, potholed street to reach my mobile home. When José, in uniform, opened the door for me, I found he already had a passenger—a friend of mine, one of the few in this largely conservative area to join me in speaking out against the war. "You're not the only one to ride in this limo today," he said, laughing.

When we arrived at the NBC station, we were somewhat amused to discover that, since the station produced no local newscasts, there was no news set available. So they had to improvise. I was to sit on a chair perched on top of a wooden box. As I was being assisted onto my "throne," I felt a wave of panic—what if I lost my balance and tumbled off during the live telecast? The interview was conducted by Bryant Gumbel, and I was surprised to learn that Courty Bryan would be joining us from a studio in New Hartford, Connecticut. The program went well.

"Mrs. Mullen," Gumbel asked, "does the inevitability of friendly fire deaths in any way help you come to grips with the loss of a loved one?"

"Not at all," I replied, "you don't ever come to grips with the loss of a loved one. You don't make that long, endless ride to an airport to pick up a flag-draped coffin and ever forget—or ever believe there was a reason."

Gumbel continued: "What did you think when you heard about the latest friendly fire tragedies?"

"Of course it's going to happen," I reflected. "The figures were so high in Vietnam—probably 10,000 out of 58,000. This is just the beginning—I'm sure there will be massive friendly fires because of military hardware. We've sold our hardware around the world, so we'll be fighting our own guns, tanks, and fighter planes. Along with the sand, confusion will become massive. Friendly fires will be obscene."

Gumbel was anxious to correct my figures and said, "The 10,000 you mentioned included all nonhostile deaths." He turned to Courty Bryan, "Mr. Bryan, do you see any difference between Vietnam and now, in the way the Pentagon handles the friendly fire deaths?"

"The major difference is the openness in which the army handled this," Bryan said. "They certainly didn't do that when Peg's son died in Vietnam."

"What is the procedure now for handling these deaths?" Gumbel continued.

"Peg really touched an enormous change in the way these deaths were handled. Peg was determined to find the cause of her son's death, and she raised holy hell until the army told her. It is coincidental that General Schwarzkopf was Sergeant Mullen's colonel in Vietnam. I'm sure this has made him sensitive to the issue of letting parents know how their child has died in the war."

"Americans are supporting the Gulf War in overwhelming numbers. Does this surprise you?" Gumbel asked Bryan.

"I'm surprised and amazed. Let's stop kidding ourselves. We are there for oil. In the beginning we supported the Vietnam War. As the war goes on, how long will we support it?"

Gumbel turned to me: "Mrs. Mullen?"

"I find it hard to believe that the support is there. I don't know anyone who supports it. I believe it was in 1968 when the Vietnam War began to fall apart. We were there for oil, but the government didn't talk about it. We didn't want the Russians to get it. We wiped out Vietnam to save it—now they struggle to exist. It could happen all over again.

"I like to think of Iwo Jima, an eight-square-mile island bombed for seventy-four days during World War II. Yet when we put our men on the beach we lost over six thousand marines and army. Look at the land today—they are dug in with no resupply. It could happen here."

As Gumbel closed the interview he said: "We can only hope you're wrong, Mrs. Mullen."

The TV monitor was off in the studio when a familiar voice came over the air: "Hello, Peg, this is Mike Gartner."

At that moment, I knew why I had been asked to appear. Michael Gartner had been editor of the *Des Moines Register* during the Vietnam War years and had taken a stand against the war, which afforded me a great deal of access to his newspaper. Now, two decades later, he had become senior editor of the NBC News Department.

As war fever continued to build across the country, I began to have doubts about my feelings concerning the general. Had I become paranoid? Was it an obsession with me to try to destroy the man because my son had died under his command?

I decided to contact four junior officers from Michael's unit in Vietnam, three of whom had been in touch with Gene and me twenty-one years ago. I had to know how they felt today. Were they still bitter? Had they managed to exorcise their demons? I actually located all but one young officer, who seemed to have fallen through the cracks. I first contacted two mothers to learn if their sons would be willing to visit with me. The first woman I called assured me that her son would be happy to talk to me, and she gave me his phone number. When I asked for his help with my dilemma, the veteran replied: "Mrs. Mullen, you are so right. Everything you heard and everything you believe about the general's behavior in Vietnam is right on target—only far worse than you know."

The second mother I reached in Boston was quick to tell me she was sure that her son was still having the same problems today that he'd come home with in the seventies. The bitterness and hate he had for the general had never left him, only worsened during the Gulf War. I wrote to him, but he refused to answer my letter. Another sent word through a friend to go easy on Schwarzkopf, saying that he had recently written a book on his own experiences serving under him, but when he learned that Schwarzkopf had become the top general of the U.S. Army, he was afraid to go public with it.

At this writing, it has been more than three years since hostilities were brought to an abrupt end by President Bush. The oil-well fires have been smothered in Kuwait—Saddam Hussein remains in power. The U.S. military remains in the desert, with units coming and going to give protection to the Kuwaiti government. We were promised that all our military personnel would vacate the Middle East by June of 1991. Peace continues to elude the people of Kuwait.

For weeks after the truce, we heard horror stories about our military's performance in the area: the massive killing of civilians in misdirected bombing, the tragic news that about 65 percent of our combat losses were due to friendly fire (some now say that the figure is closer to 100 percent), and the English fathers and mothers wanting an answer as to why their sons died at the hands of our military in more friendly fire incidents. There were accounts of U.S. troops pushing live and dead Iraqi soldiers into trenches and burying them as our tanks rumbled over the trenches on their race toward Baghdad. The military objective of this barbaric maneuver was to intimidate the enemy and expedite their surrender. The distinguished syndicated columnist James Reston, during an interview on CBS's *Night Watch*, characterized the Gulf War as the cruelest action ever conducted by the United States government.

Throughout the years, I continued to discuss Vietnam and read book after book on the subject (with difficulty). I often wondered what the next generation would make of it. Then I received a letter that eased my concern.

In November of 1985 a call came from Phil Straw, a young professor at the University of Maryland. He explained that he was teaching an honors course under the English Department and that his subject was the Vietnam War. He was eager to point out that he himself was a veteran of the war and probably one of the few who had earned a doctorate degree.

Straw asked if I would address his class via telephone, and I readily agreed. We scheduled the hookup for 10 A.M. on November 11, Veterans Day. It was an interesting session, during which I attempted to field a number of questions posed by the students. I felt the hour passed too quickly. Teachers like Phil Straw will keep the Vietnam story alive.

In October 1991 I heard from one of Straw's students, who gave me some insight into how the course had been conducted. On the first day of class, Straw distributed bookmarks to the students. Each bookmark contained the name of the student's "best friend"—someone who had died in Vietnam. At the start of every class, Straw would tell the story of one of the "best friends" and hand out information on that person. The students were then free to do what they wanted with this material. The young student who wrote me, of course, had drawn Michael as his "best friend." "Having pored through all that material I felt compelled to write you. I want you to know that your son, Michael, is remembered."

# EPILOGUE : MICHAEL'S LETTERS HOME

Nearly all the letters Michael wrote from Vietnam have been saved. Reviewing them now after more than twenty years, I find that they reveal subtle changes his experiences wrought over a short period—a bitterness, weariness, and sense of futility.

During the years that Courty Bryan spent in writing *Friendly Fire* we had many discussions about the behavior and personality of Michael's company commander. Courty always defended Colonel Schwarzkopf, contending that he didn't take command of the 198th until December 1, 1969. More than two decades later, the sudden change in the activities of Michael's unit at that time jumps off the pages at me. He writes of the ceaseless humping, of always being tired, never getting to rest or dry out, and putting up with the "bullshit" that was growing worse than that back in the States. All of this occurred when the majority of U.S. combat units in Vietnam were being held back to save lives and to force the ARVN to take over the war. In discussing this upsurge of action with veterans who survived the 198th, we came to the conclusion it was the result of the colonel's need for body count, the Americal's requirement for promotion.

Editing these letters has been the most difficult part of this project. On rereading them, I can feel Michael searching for a way out of his predicament, although he occasionally chided me for sending him information on how others managed to get out of combat duty in Vietnam.

I noticed that he closed his final note with "hang loose," a phrase used frequently by the men in Vietnam. I had to smile at the thought that it had taken Michael almost six months to catch on to the phrase—so typical of him! Closer to the end, it seems, he talked a lot about coming home.

Michael's letters home were published in their entirety in the *Des Moines Register* on Sunday, March 29, 1970. My decision to republish them here was made when I realized that the majority of readers may know little about the Vietnam War, and many will have forgotten it.

The young people of this country lived through a year of the Persian Gulf War—seeing only a sanitized version on the TV screen, with continual propaganda that unquestioning patriotism was once again alive and well.

There is no glamour to be found in these letters home. Although they cover less than six months, they actually reflect a ten-year period of gaining ground, losing ground, and losing thousands of lives in a lost cause. I include them here in an attempt to show what war is really all about. Young soldiers in battle do not think of the flag, patriotism, or their government—they are concerned with saving their own skin and that of their friends.

### SEPTEMBER 23

Just another day. We had classes all morning with more this afternoon. They entailed booby traps and rather hairy.

If you send stuff, make sure it is a small box and can be easily carried . . . food like M&M's peanuts go good here. Went through finance here and literally scream each time I do it. I mentioned in my last letter that if the bank didn't get the $60 allotment for July to keep in mind that I am charged for it. Please check for months of June, July, August, and September. Now as to bonds, a $50 and $25 should come every three months. Keep track of them and if they don't arrive, please make inquiry. Why all the bother? Because I am billed for them here and if they don't arrive there, the Army says it has paid, so you know who is shorted. They tell me that it's the bank's problem.

Would appreciate a front page once in a while to read. You don't get news here if you don't have a radio and I don't want to drag one around. Today is hot and sticky. There aren't any real easy jobs over here . . . it is a 24-hour day, seven days a week. See that Nixon finally got around to moving a few out. The bay here is rather beautiful, large and blue.

### SEPTEMBER 24

Today we spent at a firebase reviewing several weapons. Then the troops fired a few rounds . . . thus the day was short. Of course, all time is guard time. We traveled around the base and it is quite large, like shanty town. We have a short class tonight on the starlite scope. Have had it three times before. I have four days more of classes. My unit is about 15 miles northwest of Chu Lai and pulls short patrols and guards the area north of Chu Lai. Expect later we will be reassigned to another area.

### SEPTEMBER 28

I am at Firebase Bayonet, which is just outside Chu Lai. Will move out to my company tomorrow about noon. It is a platoon with about 25 men, one 2nd lieutenant and one E-5 like myself. The area where I will be moving is probably one of the better places over here. I believe I got a break for a change—but know full well nothing here, even a base camp, is a good haul.

Have two E-5 friends in D Company, so things are pretty good. Need only a few things, (a) leather shoe strings, 4 pairs, (b) 2 rolls of fishing line, nylon, no questions. Need them for things you wouldn't understand.

OCTOBER 2

Have received your package with two letters and dad's comment. Please check allotments, send shoe laces and nylon fishing lines. The monsoons are here and it is raining for a week straight now, so have been wet for a week. Here is what I need. Something that I can wear under my fatigues to keep warm and dry—it must be lightweight.

OCTOBER 5

Today I got a rubber wet suit—they keep you dry, but you sweat yourself wet. Maybe nylon tights might keep me warm. Need only something for my legs. As for food, don't send anything that can't be eaten in one sitting. Now, what am I doing? We set up each day in an area called a day logger, put up tentlike hutches to keep out of rain. Then at night we are given places to check out—you could call these night squad patrols to a certain area and then move out. Now, what are we really doing? We move out at about 7 to an area that we checked in the afternoon and set up a platoon perimeter and sit out the night. In this way our lieutenant is not playing the game—when you have 70 grunts on your back, it is hard to keep things under control.

OCTOBER 8

Same ole stuff—am drying socks over a peanut butter jar. Repeat, I need the shoe strings and fishing line. Don't send any more wash pads. Things are uptight. We get anywhere from two to four 'copters a day, one for "C" rations, another for resupply of equipment and mail, maybe one for a hot meal and always one to get junk out of here.

The area we're in is what they call the southern rocket pocket south of Chu Lai. We are to protect Chu Lai from rockets by finding them. This is the job of the 1-6th, which is just one battalion in the 198th. Others are 196th up north and 11th at Doc Phu. Last night our platoon went out and set up an ambush away from our day camp. This gives us pretty good security since all VC elements here are of small nature most of the time.

As I said, we are resupplied every day, clean clothes once a week. The hardest part is to find out what you need to carry and dump the non-essentials. Right now I am under my poncho tent—have my socks drying over the peanut butter jar. Mom, did you receive the money I sent home? Should be a Treasury check, so buy a time certificate with it.

OCTOBER 10

To the Jensens [close family friends]: From reading you know that many of these people live in a primitive way in thatched huts with dirt floors and personal hygiene is non-existent, so you can imagine the real trouble over here. Also another problem, many GI's, because of bitterness and frustration, are cruel and inhumane to these people, and this causes much trouble. For over here you don't know who your enemy really is, every Vietnamese becomes a suspected enemy, and the GI has the belief, better me alive and him dead instead of taking a chance. It is all too complex to explain in a few words. Suppose you hate to see winter come with all the snow. Yet, a little snow would be appreciated by me. Must be going now.

OCTOBER 16

Only have a minute to say "hi." Am going to mountains for a spell and have to hump everything. Am in 1st platoon (198th) and have an ROTC Lt. giving orders by the book and the book doesn't mean a damn thing here.

OCTOBER 22

Just got out of the mountains. Will bring you up to date. Our area of operations is close to Chu Lai but secondary area is west and into mountains. On Sunday the operations major set up a search and destroy mission into the villages [at this time the administration was telling us that our ground troops were not on the offensive]. We swept down a valley and then up a mountain and found a small grenade-mine factory, which we destroyed. Continued up the mountains. Took all afternoon and into next morning. My company had one edge of mountain, another company had the other side and ARVN in the valley.

Sunday morning we moved out and ran into a rear guard of NVA. I had one boy injured. We kept going and stayed on top—I must have fallen a dozen times. Then linked up with the other company and the ARVN left us. We swept into a valley that had not been cleared—about 4:30 our 'copter drew fire—found a village under the trees with about a mile to go. While at the river getting water, a VC unit tried to hit our rear, but we knocked them out.

Further down our platoon killed three buffalo which the villagers had turned loose. Our platoon was first in movement that day and my squad first. We moved into the village about 7 P.M. and stayed until 2 A.M. Down the road a captured momason told of a hardcore VC village. We pounded it for three hours (middle of night) with artillery and then for about two more hours with a "Spooky" DC-3 with machine guns. About dawn we burned out the village—burned the other village also.

We were 'coptered out at 8 A.M. and are now five miles south of Chu Lai in a rocket pocket—back to safe (?) ambushes. Well, anyway you can see that we continue to have search and destroy missions.

Am glad to see that the president is having some pressure put on him, but am sure he will just turn away. You can see here they are trying like hell to get all divisions up to full strength, at least in our area, on the whole the entire mess is a joke. I don't believe the NVA wants to fight. The American ground troops have slowed up too, with less stress on long missions. The area I am in has a lot of rice, and that is important. But it is a pipe dream to think you can bring these people up to time in a couple of years. They are 200 years behind.

OCTOBER 25

Today is as good as last night was bad. Yesterday we moved out and were to meet the platoon sergeant at a rally point, for he had been on patrol all afternoon. When we met we disagreed as to where we were and moved out to our ambush sites. Then about 9:30 an aerial burst, which is called a marking round, went off 100 meters to our rear. Then all hell broke loose on our left front and I got on the horn calling in and after 2½ hours of figuring came to conclusion we were 1,000 meters too far east—moved at midnight.

These are the kind of mistakes you read about. The maps are not accurate, trails shown on map where there are no trails, and actual trails in bush not shown on map. We were victim of a trail that was new and the trail on our map was further west, anyway, it's a tough ball game. Today, we got beer, soda and hot chow. Am enclosing

Howard's note. Get a kick out of this trans-Pacific mail. Laughed at the peace thing of the 15th. I'm afraid they don't know Nixon—Nixon can't be pushed.

Another day gone by. It rained last night and this morning. It has stopped but looks like it will pitter-patter all day. Really enjoyed the papers. We are supposed to have the colonel out here sometime this week. Have to laugh at them for they live in a dream world. They have to have figures (body count) and nobody knows what is a VC or a plain ignorant villager, at least in this area. Have my tennis shoes on, feel comfortable but have a sore heel. Using a shoe lace to hold up the poncho. We go back north on Thursday—is a little better area. So til later, hang on.

OCTOBER 27

Finished a note this morning but that was before mail came in. Received yours of the 22nd on the 27th, usually five to seven days. Also got a note from Pat, letter with pictures from the Jensens. The last month the 198th has been looking for hidden supplies and this might account for the news as we found some stuff in the mountains last week.

Got newspapers and appreciate them. Glad to see that my bonds came through. As to my money here, it stays here, about $180 a month. It was too time-consuming and bothersome to make out new allotments and they take two months to go into effect. Now, they just keep a running log of my pay and I draw out $20 a month. No interest, but then no time, no worry and no mistakes.

If you and dad want to get me a small Christmas gift try a cheap luminous Timex—but make sure it is waterproof—the one I have is not and is almost useless.

OCTOBER 31

We came out of southern area and back to our Basecamp Bayonet next to Chu Lai. Have had a real sore foot for a week, to the extent of being able only to hop along. Finally got to a first aid station and have blisters under callouses. Am enclosing my pay voucher receipt – guard it! Will be here all day and what a pleasure to get three hot meals and a cold beer. Really believe Nixon is in a bind—if he comes up short on continued slowing down of the war, the pressure will be on again. He certainly can't use more of that.

NOVEMBER 1

Dear Mrs. Jensen: The weather today has taken a turn for the best. The sun has come out and things are drying out. Will work in the same general area for a couple days, which means less humping than normal. See that politics are warming up at home with VP getting on TV a lot. Makes for interesting reading.

If you have followed the papers, you would have read about the mess in Quang Nagi Province near me—murdering a village, etc. A lot of the paper stuff was overblown and mostly rumors were published. But there were some individuals in the area over a year ago, that is true, but out of time and circumstance things take on a different complexion.

NOVEMBER 3

Same old day here, rained last night. In fact, started to rain the minute I got back to the field, if that means anything. We are north of Chu Lai, about six miles and about two miles from the coast. Mostly small villages here. Land is rather flat with rice paddies. We have two more weeks out in the field before we go into a three-day rest at basecamp. Was back at the camp for over two days on account of blisters; was a welcome break. Don't have anymore to say. Just keep the steaks in the freezer and have John align the front end of the purple Ford.

NOVEMBER 4

Received your note of the 20th and had to laugh at [mother's] impression of Nixon and especially after listening to his speech this morning. Then he ended with more promises, if—if—if? I believe Hugh Scott and a few of the others who had made comments have to swallow a little, for Nixon used them. I believe he will be forced to act—don't think Mansfield will be so kind now.

Today, raining as usual and we are in a large open valley, all scrub bushes and no trees. I'm on the ground on an air mattress. Papers came today. Thanks.

NOVEMBER 9

Today is Sunday. Received a camera from Howard. Planned to carry it, but our concept of operations has been changed from night ambushes to day patrolling, which means walking and I hate to carry it around and get it hung up here and there. Got a note from Sgt. Cornu, a buddy from McClellan, and he is at Pleiku. Have had no action there in a month. They keep saying here that things will open soon, but they don't really know where, except that things northwest of Saigon have picked up. No mail today!

NOVEMBER 11

Got your note of the 5th. Raining as usual. Will answer your questions. Too much bother to make another allotment. Will lose $50—$75 interest but it would take two months to take effect and in all honesty will be home by June. I have been through enough Army financial centers.

As for Nixon's vietnamization—it will eventually fail, our front-line troops here have little faith in the ARVN. In our area the coastal plain is about five miles from the sea to the mountains. Right now the VC are coming down at night into the villages and trying to get them back, and there is little we can do. That is why we are running night ambushes and will start patrolling more.

As to the wristwatch, yes, we are supposed to get them but they are long gone before they get down to our level.

As to morale, had to laugh at Westmoreland's statement. Most of the troops (grunts), E-6's and below, are hoping that things get wilder at home. They may not agree with the demonstrations, and most feel in our area they are wasting their time. Militarily, I kind of agree that all hell is going to break loose after Christmas and Nixon will be on a tack.

So much for the bad stuff. For the next three days we are to guard a bridge (Tam Ky) and fill sandbags, which beats sleeping on the ground. Then we go in for a three-day rest called standdown. You must check to see how much I have in my checking account. Glad to see that Mr. Saylor is getting his payment. Have used the camera—will take a few more while on the bridge and try somehow to send film home.

NOVEMBER 17

Have only a moment—all is well. We are in third day of standdown and move out tomorrow. Has been a decent two days. Ran into a buddy from NCO at division headquarters. Had to get a pair of glasses and ran into him at the PX. Got a letter from Pat, Louise and your candy yesterday, so all is uptight. The rain has let up the last two days, but we can swim anyway. Mom, write more than just a letter to the kid.

NOVEMBER 19

Have been too busy to hop a note this week. Received your letter with clippings and only comment being that you must be the vocal minority, seems like the silent majority has the upper hand now. We are off standdown now, back out in the field. Am getting newspapers pretty regular now. We will be pulling night ambushes for a while. Weather pretty good. Didn't rain last night.

NOVEMBER 23

Received your note and laughed again because Agnew felt strong enough to take on the *Times* and *Post.* I should think Nixon would be suffering now, and as for Haynesworth, they got him where it hurts. The Democrats desperately need a fighter now to get the ball rolling. I can't imagine why there isn't someone to move forward.

So far the only bullshit has been north of us toward Danang. There is to be a big battalion operation in two days, so will be flying again soon. Got moved out two days ago as a gunship was fired at. We found a small complex and killed two of them. We went in after the aerial bombardment and checked out the few tunnels. Just a normal day.

NOVEMBER 28

Too busy to write the past few days, although things are rather quiet. Wish they would stay that way. We feel there is a slight chance that our battalion will be in the withdrawal after Christmas. If I have less than six months will be sent to another battalion.

Doing lots of humping lately. We humped with third platoon this A.M. and are sweeping the valley. Now we are sitting on top of a hill acting as a blocking force. Received your watch today, thanks. But damn, it is not a luminous dial so no good for night ambushes. Am enclosing another voucher—be sure and file it away. Am thankful that I am seeing E-5 pay when I see what some of the boys are paid.

Right now they (headquarters) are having the usual confusion of coordinating three platoons. They want to have a fire mission, and of course, have to clear an area. It is a great wonder this army moves as well as it does.

DECEMBER 2

Humped out yesterday as a blocking force and back last night. This afternoon we get resupplied for a three-day mission so you won't be hearing from me. Could you send me some canned orange or grapefruit juice?

As to papers, you are sending too much—desire only front section and sports; seems a waste of money to send want ads at today's prices. Right now am waiting for the hot chow bird—it is late. Have to get my boots back on now; really appreciate the tennis shoes as they allow my shoes and feet to dry out. I would really like some "real gold" orange juice.

DECEMBER 6 OR 7

Lying under poncho in the sun. Just heard that Texas beat Arkansas. Have had plenty of mail today and yesterday. Have been doing a lot of humping lately, but for next three days will be in the same area.

You mentioned the mess in Quang Nagi Province. You've got to remember this is an area that is strongly VC and even today the 11th Division operating there is constantly running into booby traps, etc. You will find that the thing was ballooned all out of proportion as to what actually happened. In this case, Agnew was right. If you can send a plastic unbreakable comb, I would appreciate it, along with a small mirror for shaving. One that will survive lots of abuse. Am waiting for food; hope it makes it in one piece.

DECEMBER 9

Rather cold today. Listened to Nixon and his press conference; glad to see that more troops will be leaving. I don't think it will be this brigade, but the Americal will lose one unit, most likely. Got your cookies today; right amount and right container. Am glad you're checking on my monthly allotments, and would appreciate it if you lumped my savings and checking accounts for another time certificate. The last couple of days have been lazy and I hope they stay that way. Our 2nd platoon took off into the mountains on a recon sweep and are eventually working back this way. To my back are the mountains, about two miles away. Keep the mail coming.

DECEMBER 14

Only 11 days of shopping til Christmas. Days are getting long; we now have to dig in each morning and this takes about three hours. Today my hole ended at two feet and the rocks were bigger than I am. Things in this area are getting chicken shit, to say the least. I'm afraid things are going to open up after Christmas; these are two-level intelligence reports. Kind of wonder if the high-ups will say anything about it.

Am tired right now, sitting next to my foxhole, which is facing into a hedgerow. The stupidity of it all sort of makes me laugh at times. We still have the rainy season with us. Don't have more to say, but write!

DECEMBER 16

Got your note of the 8th along with nuts and bread; both were really appreciated. Today is rain as usual, and we are now required to dig in during the day, a foxhole and a sleeping hole which makes for a mess with mud, and it takes more of the morning. We move out at 3 P.M. to another location and dig in again. Right now our platoon is with the mortar platoon. They have had their ammo requirements raised and we have to hump in the extra.

Glad to see all is well, and Mom, I might add you are becoming more like Grandma with your politics. As for the 198th, it is made up of three battalions; 1-6th, 1-52, 1-46 with the 1-6 protecting Chu Lai, which makes us last to go in the brigade. Now the Americal Division is made up of three brigades—196th between Chu Lai and Danang, 198th at Chu Lai and the 11th at Doc Phu, which is the brigade in which Mylai, or Pinksville, lies and is south of here.

In this brigade the 1-52 is slated to leave first. Read in the paper where Fred Friendly commented on Agnew's TV speech and he seemed to think it did have some merit. Would appreciate it if you would let me know what my account amounts to now, and if over $500 buy certificates.

DECEMBER 17

Same place, same hole—6 days of rain. We didn't get resupplied yesterday so am waiting for food. No birds in air today, all grounded. The roll of film that is good probably shows a day logger in the pines, plus a few birds and couple of huts. Now, we have to stay on the ground and dig in—mud and all. Nixon is to pull out 50,000, he said yesterday. Will affect this division and the 196th, with the 1-52 to go first.

To get resupplied we have to depend on the 17th Cavalry, and their tracks today. Am not carrying the camera, too much weight and too hard on camera. The area around here is small, knoll-type hills with brush and rice paddies in village. Have a ridge of mountains to west. My letters have been evident, have been on three-day missions the last month, nothing but patrolling an area, and no resupply during the period.

DECEMBER 22

Sorry I haven't been able to write, but we are moving all day, digging in at night, and pulling a heavy guard, so little time to do it. Received your cookies and Mary's package today. Nuts were good. About allotments, wait til Jan. 7 and if they have not come by then, send me notarized statement to the effect and I will make a trip to finance during standdown around 13–15 of January. Drop a note to Marilyn thanking her for my Christmas package. Also thank Rosauer's and Skinney for their cards. My letters will depend on luck for a while, it looks like. We are running company-size sweeps and that means walking. Can't say much more other than Christmas is only a couple days away or another way of saying only eight months left in this hell-hole.

DECEMBER 25

It is Christmas and all is well. We are even going to stay put. The sun came out and we had Mass. The battalion commander was here, so I guess we rate above average. Have a couple of cards to write so this will be short. Expect winter is thick and heavy snow by now.

Received the round can of candy today, so was a good present. Tell Pat I don't have time to write now, with this humping in the daytime. Look forward to getting out of this place by June. Things are up in the air, nobody knows anything except that activity is slowly picking up, and people have their fingers crossed. Keep the newspapers coming—really enjoy them. Many times I do believe they are better than food.

DECEMBER 30

Am well, kicking and so tired. Has rained the last couple of days; we did stop yesterday to rest. Have received your last two packages, fudge and cookies. Our area of operations has been enlarged and we are humping more and enjoying it less. Have just two weeks til our three-day standdown. Saw where Iowa beat Drake.

JANUARY 3

Am tired and no free time. Today we looked for a downed plane. Missing two months, and found it located over about 80 acres. Kind of anxious to see if we will be affected by withdrawal. Am enclosing pay voucher. Hope all is well.

JANUARY 3

Dear Jensens: Hope all is well. Things have been long as of late, long hours, bad weather, etc. Would trade things for a little snow. Sorry I don't write more often, but the last months have been hectic. Be good.

JANUARY 4

Today we are resting. Last night our Firebase Bayonet got hit and mainly because our battalion commander has his companies too damn far out, and as a result we are being airlifted back to base, and pull bunker guard at least until standdown. Has winter let up any? It doesn't feel right to be laying in the mud here and not cold. My papers have not been coming through, last being the 16th. Watch the allotments.

JANUARY 10

We are still on bunker line, but we move off tomorrow for three-day mission before standdown. We have been here for a week, which is a break. Had a three-day reprieve from the rain, but it is raining again now. Got your last package yesterday so am uptight. It was about the right size. Hope winter is letting up a little.

Glad to see the allotments are catching up. Don't want to lose a dime over this war. As things look now, the Americal will not be involved in the next big withdrawal, will be the Big Red and a brigade or two from other units. Glad to hear that Cecil's better.

JANUARY 16

All is well—am in second day of standdown and all is bullshit. In fact, made up my mind to apply for an early out, and to get out by May 25. Am now a platoon sergeant—the bullshit is getting worse, almost as bad as stateside. After standdown am going on another company into the hills. Had to laugh about the pullout—looks good to bring the Big Red home, but they aren't doing shit now anyway. Feel nobody knows about the Americal Division—although it is the largest in 'Nam—26,000.

Am rather tired this standdown—if all works out, will have only two more to go. Have less time to write than ever before. Got your popcorn package today. You mentioned Tam Ky—yes if the film turned out, the bridge pictured is Tam Ky, a coastal town on Highway 1. The dinks are coming out of the hills in small groups. They are getting bold of late. Two days ago we walked through an area where the VC had been staying—was a rest area along the river—right in the middle of our area of operation.

Have been fighting a supply problem of late—seems now that the ARVN has top priority on all items. Things in the rear are a mess.

JANUARY 21

Am well. Have been hiking since standdown but have been staying in the same place at night. Hiked four checks today, may be short, but the rice paddies get to you.

At standdown finance came and made a note about the $60.00 missing. I couldn't get up to the main finance center to draw out $453. Have already written to Doc O'Dell at University of Missouri.

To set things straight—the VC here are small seldom seen. Last time we saw any was Nov. 17. Our company last made contact 10 days ago—one sniper. They are here and sometimes we are just hours behind, like about 10 days ago. But things are subject to change. Five from our platoon did see Bob Hope at Chu Lai—flown in. We hump up a hill tomorrow looking for caves—are next to a large village complex. Keep the papers coming. Got to go.

JANUARY 23

We are on the bunker line now for a short spell during Tet. Recently we moved out of the Northern Rocket Pocket. We were gone just one hour when the dinks threw nine rockets at Chu Lai. We were picked up and flown back—had to sweep a hill—2nd platoon ran into three VC and lost two, but we got them. The rocket sticks were just a hill behind our patrol base. My unit came out unhurt—walked in. Will be here til middle of February. Hope all is well at home. Papers about two weeks behind but they're appreciated. Hope to hear from Doc O'Dell soon.

FEBRUARY 1

You would never believe it, but it has been rather cold. We are on the bunker line at Bayonet near Chu Lai. Things are rather quiet, but they say will pick up—but you never know. Got paid yesterday but $60 correction hasn't caught up yet and am enclosing voucher. Right now we are supposed to be building bunkers, but being typical Army, have no materials, no tools—same old story. Bye.

FEBRUARY 2

Received your note of the 27th. Let's get one thing straight, Mom. For God's sake, stop the worrying bit. Will you! If you worry, don't write about it. As for those two chicken shits—it seems if they weren't happy in their jobs they can get out of them if they wanted to bad enough. I've seen too many of these soft, smart kids writing home congressmen and senators and Mama, too. I have no stomach for their type. The main problem in this mess is nobody wants to do his job and do it the best he can.

Now to try for an early out—should not be hard to do—one E-5 in our company had no trouble in getting one for night school.

All it took was a letter of acceptance. Yes, I got the scotch. I can't get to finance and I don't worry about it, not important. The last couple of days we have been building bunkers on the out perimeter or Bayonet. It is a leisurely type of life, work some, rest and sleep and, of course, pull guard. Ran into a boy from Waterloo by name of Culpepper. The weather here of late has been cold and wintery, but not like home.

FEBRUARY 7

All is well, have a dry bed. Got a letter from O'Dell. All is O.K. Also got a letter from University of Missouri admission office. Have sent in my enrollment card—should be an acceptance in about three weeks. Wrote a check for $410 to Missouri so cover it with some of my money. Also bought a tape recorder for $234, so cover it also. Will take six to eight weeks to get home.

FEBRUARY 11

We are still at bunker line. Will be here a couple more days. Will move out on a search mission for a week. The weather is holding reasonably well. Last card I mentioned that I had written a check to Missouri and they would send me the papers needed. Now I have bought a small recorder from the PX, $234—it should arrive between 45 to 60 days. It is a fair recorder, decided not to take an R and R as I will try to get out of here by June, and mine isn't scheduled until May anyway.

FEBRUARY 11

Pat: All is well—got your Cutty Sark—but it broke crossing a river so wasn't able to indulge in it completely. See that winter has been rather tough. Also football politics interesting at Iowa. Hope Iowa keeps winning—they desperately need a winner of some sort. Have to run.

FEBRUARY 11

Dear Jensens: Received your note and glad to see that the Jensens are surviving the crazy winter. Sort of takes you back to 1936, ha! With luck, will be home by June—I'm trying for an early out for school. Sincerely hope I can get it.

Things have been rather quiet of late and hope they stay that way. We have been on bunker guard at Bayonet. Next week we go back into the field and go to work for the next six weeks. Till then, be well and healthy.

FEBRUARY 13

Went down off the hill, bunker line, to get a haircut and clean up, but ended up hitching a ride to Chu Lai. Went to the Mars station by chance. They were open and not busy, so got a chance to call. Suppose it was midnight at home and guess you were surprised. Went from there to finance and drew out $561 and sent it home via express checks. Wish you to put it in the bank. Will keep the stubs til checks reach home. Will be on the bunker about two more days, then back into the field. Glad that all is well—weather here has been rather cold. When my recorder comes, I'll appreciate it not be opened but stored away til I get home. Plan to buy about $250 more equipment. Just as well do it now as later. Have decided not to take an R and R if I can get a drop.

So til later, hang loose.

SINGULAR LIVES

The Anti-Warrior: A Memoir
*By Milt Felsen*

Black Eagle Child: The Facepaint Narratives
*By Ray A. Young Bear*

Fly in the Buttermilk: The Life Story of Cecil Reed
*By Cecil Reed with Priscilla Donovan*

In My Father's Study
*By Ben Orlove*

Journey into Personhood
*By Ruth Cameron Webb*

Letters from Togo
*By Susan Blake*

A Prairie Populist: The Memoirs of Luna Kellie
*Edited by Jane Taylor Nelsen*

Taking Part: A Twentieth-Century Life
*By Robert Josephy*

Tales of an American Hobo
*By Charles Elmer Fox*

Unfriendly Fire: A Mother's Memoir
*By Peg Mullen*

The Warsaw Sparks
*By Gary Gildner*